Preventing Child Sexual Abuse In Youth-Serving Organizations

Guidelines for Managers & Parents

Norman D. Bates, Esq.
Christine Army, MA

A joint publication of

NATIONAL CRIME PREVENTION COUNCIL

LIABILITY CONSULTANTS
Since 1986

THE NATIONAL CENTER FOR Victims of Crime

sexually abusive acts may include sexual penetration, sexual touching, or non-contact sexual acts such as exposure or voyeurism."[1]

Child sexual assault as defined by National Center for Victims of Crime is the following:

"Sexual assault takes many forms including attacks such as rape or attempted rape, as well as any unwanted sexual contact or threats. Usually a sexual assault occurs when someone touches any part of another person's body in a sexual way, even through clothes, without that person's consent."[2]

These two terms most generally differ in that child sexual abuse encompasses a wider variety of acts that can include assault, the showing of pornography to a child, exposing oneself to a child, and voyeurism.

Interpreting the Data

Estimating how many children are being or have ever been sexually abused is problematic. Some of the challenges that are faced include: inconsistent state definitions of child sexual abuse, under and non-reporting, a variety of report receiving/data collecting agencies and how the data is reported.

1. Inconsistent State Definitions of Child Sexual Abuse

There is no single definition of child sexual abuse used currently. States vary in what age is considered a "child" as well as who can legally be held responsible for child sexual abuse.

2. Under and non-reporting

Many cases of child sexual abuse are not reported right away and some are never reported. Therefore, the actual number of children who are or have ever been sexually abused is currently unknown.

3. Report receiving agencies

Depending upon how a state defines child sexual abuse, usually reports will be reported to either local law enforcement or Child Protective Services (CPS). However, many instances of sexual abuse never reach these agencies and are dealt with internally by the organizations and/or individuals involved.

4. Data collecting agencies

There are a number of agencies that collect data on child sexual abuse. The National Child Abuse and Neglect Data System (NCANDS), the data collecting system of the National Data Archive on Child Abuse and Neglect (NDACAN), gathers information from participating CPS agencies. However, they do not collect data from local law enforcement. This means that current data collecting systems only capture a portion of the total incidents of CSA.

5. How the data is reported

Understanding the scope of child sexual abuse means taking into account both prevalence and incidence rates.

The number of child sexual abuse cases will be reported in one of two ways: incidence or prevalence. "Incidence rates are based on how many children were abused in a single year. Prevalence rates are based on a lifetime or a full childhood, such as what percentage of all children were ever abused."[3]

Data from the CDC in 2006 indicates that 1 in 4 women and 1 in 6 men were sexually abused before the age of 18.[4]

The data regarding child sexual abuse can be confusing. Consequently, this can lead to inconsistent data reports as shown by the following statistics.

- According to the publication "Child Maltreatment" published by NCANDS, data gathered from participating Child Protec-

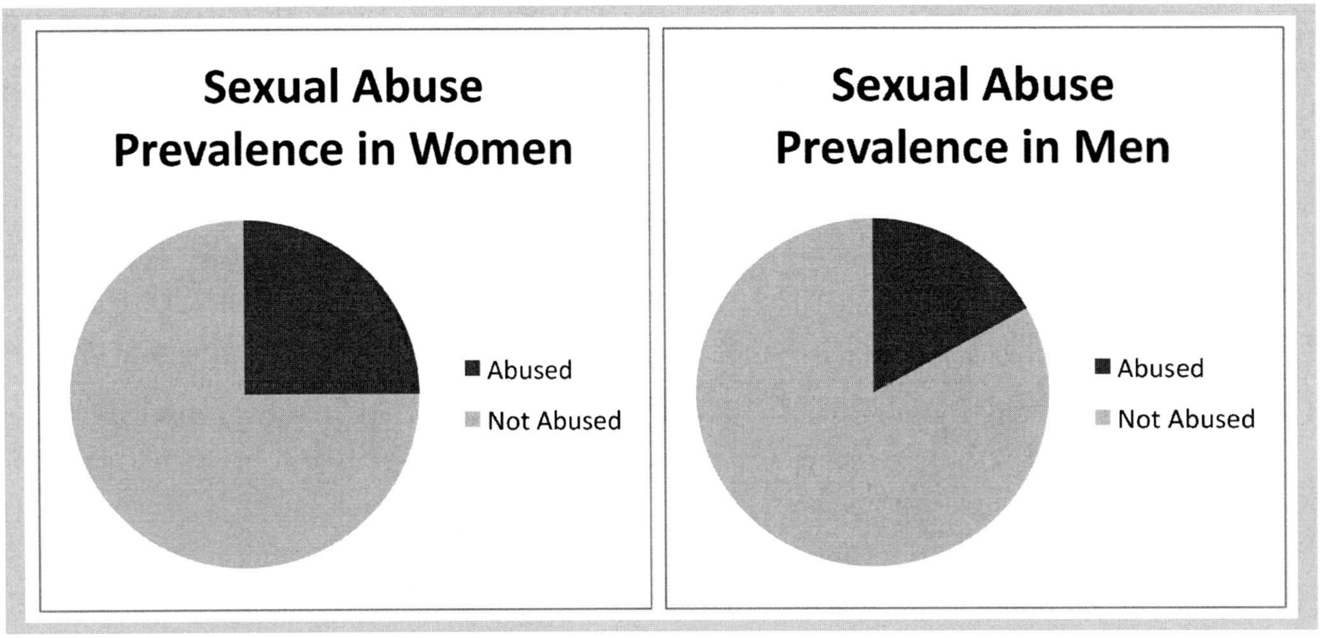

Data: CDC Study, 2006

tive Services agencies in 2011 indicates that of all cases received and screened in, 9.1% were sexual abuse cases.[5]

- In 2006, the Centers for Disease Control (CDC) conducted an adult retrospective study that estimated that 1 in 4 women (25%) and 1 in 6 men (17%) were sexually abused before the age of 18.[6]

- Prevalence rates used by some professionals in the field range from 8% to 20%.[7]

- One in 5 girls (20%) and 1 in 20 (5%) boys are the victim of child sexual abuse.[8]

- The 2003 National Institute of Justice report stated that 3 out of 4 victims (75%) of child sexual abuse have been sexually victimized by someone they knew well.[9]

- Bureau of Justice Statistics report that 1.6% of children between the ages of 12-17 are the victims of rape/sexual assault.[10]

- A 2001 National Child Victimization Survey estimates that 1.9 per 1,000 children (0.19%) aged 12-17 are raped/sexually assaulted.[11]

The severity of the incidence and prevalence of an issue often determines how much public attention and help it will receive. Before something can be fixed, the scope of the problem must be known.

I. The Scope of the Problem

With reported rates of child sexual abuse reaching anywhere from 8% to 20% of the child population under 18, the true extensiveness of the problem is unknown. When assessing rates of child sexual abuse, a number of considerations must be understood and will be discussed throughout the first portion of this publication. Issues that may arise and pose a threat to the accuracy of child sexual abuse rates include distinguishing between intra- and extra-familial sexual abuse, delays in disclosure/reporting and under-reporting, and the limited prosecution of child sexual abuse cases.

1. Intra- and Extra-Familial Sexual Abuse

The reality of child sexual abuse is that most offenders are known to their victims, including relatives and family members. According to the Bureau of Statistics, it is estimated that approximately 90% of juvenile sexual abuse victims know their perpetrator in some way. However, the first gap in research and statistics of child sexual abuse is the challenge of categorizing offenders of child sexual abuse. Part of this can be attributed to the inherent complexity and nature of human relationships. Individuals can have family members, relatives, biological and non-biological parents/relatives, close friends, friends, acquaintances, friends of the family, trusted known persons, known persons, and strangers. It is no small feat to attempt to classify each case of sexual abuse into one of these categories, and therefore the categories are often condensed for purposes of simplicity. Some studies condense the categories of offenders to "known" versus "stranger", while others attempt to elaborate and separate offenders into categories of relative/family member, acquaintance, and stranger.

The lack of uniformity about how to characterize offenders leads to poor estimates of the perpetrator data for child sexual abuse. Within the data analysis, how to distinguish a trusted coach who is a "friend of the family" from a worker at a local youth organization, who does not share a similar relationship to the family, remains an enigma. Because most child sexual abuse occurs within the family, traditional research may place less importance on the other categories of victim/offender relationships. This may be why the data for intra-familial child sexual abuse is more thorough than that for extra-familial child sexual abuse.

However, attention has shifted in recent years as a result of numerous child sexual abuse scandals reported by the press. The media has highlighted the need to be aware of individuals who are not immediately related to the child or are acquaintances of the family, but who may be working with the child in another capacity such as a coach, teacher, day care worker, or youth volunteer.

This publication will highlight some youth-serving organizations where the extra-familial relationships can be found. Substantial efforts are being made within these organizations to combat CSA. The organizations discussed include the Boy Scouts of America (BSA), YMCA, the Amateur Athletic Union (AAU), Big Brothers Big Sisters of America, and the Boys and Girls Club of America.

2. Disclosure of the Abuse

In addition to facing categorization difficulties, data regarding child sexual abuse is also skewed because of delayed disclosure or non-disclosure. Consequently, the exact number of children who are sexually abused annually is difficult to estimate. Yet, according to the Darkness to Light organization, "even if the true prevalence of child abuse is not known, most professionals agree that there will be 500,000 babies in the US this year that will be sexually abused before they turn 18 if steps are not taken to prevent it."[12]

While the concept of non-disclosure poses a problem similar to that of delayed disclosure, the term "disclosure" itself lacks a clear and concise definition among researchers. *Disclosure* in this publication means the victim making sexual abuse public.

One of the main factors in whether children decide to disclose incidences of sexual abuse has primarily to do with who they are reporting it to and how likely those people are to believe what the children are saying. Parents should therefore maintain and create comfortable communication between themselves and their children. Studies have shown that "more than half of all child abuse incidents are never reported because the victims are too afraid or too confused to be able to report their experiences."[13]

As a result of the fear of disclosing, the average age of disclosure of child sexual abuse is around 25 years, and only one-third of those sexually abused disclosed it before the age of 18. This is called *delayed disclosure*, and is often linked with repressed memories and other illnesses stemming from the abuse. *Delayed disclosures* are often difficult to substantiate because of the time that has elapsed between the sexual abuse and the report.

The following narrative is an excerpt from a police report, which illustrates a typical delayed disclosure in a case involving child sexual abuse.

> *"Victim states that ten years ago he was sexually assaulted by a white male named [name of assailant]. Victim states that he was at a lock-in at the [YSO facility] at 30 Main Street. Victim advised that he and other juveniles were with [the assailant] when the assault occurred. [The assailant] was supposed to be a counselor in training at the [YSO]. Victim advised that there should be other victims of sexual assault from the same subject."*

3. Limited Prosecution of Offenders

Another challenge to the accuracy of child sexual abuse rates is the limited prosecution of child sexual abuse cases. For example, arrests are made in only 29% of the cases reported to the police, with arrests being made more often in incidents involving older children (32%). Arrests are made in only 19% of cases involving children under the age of 6.[14] In many cases where arrests are made, there is no prosecution.

Another possible reason for a case to not be prosecuted is the retraction of the accusation. Due to the pressure and encouragement of some adults, there are situations in which children will take back their accusations. There are a number of possible reasons why parents or guardians would pressure children into retracting their statements. One of the main reasons is that parents are concerned that their child would suffer more if made to go through an investigation and trial. This is often done on "behalf of the child," so as not to put them through additional trauma.

Another reason for there to be no prosecution may be a lack of sufficient evidence. It is for this reason that reporting, interviewing, and investigative protocols are crucially important. They may be the difference between prosecuting the crime or not.

The reported number of child sexual abuse incidents is therefore lower than the actual frequency. This is due to cases being dropped, unsubstantiated, or retracted, even though the crime may have occurred.

Reporting sexual abuse is difficult and complex. There may be a number of reasons why a child withholds this information. A few examples cited by victims are shame and guilt, fear of backlash, not being "heard" or understood, getting in trouble or the fear of getting in trouble, poor communication with the adults in their lives, fear of repeat victimization, being threatened by the offender, and being in a position where contact with the offender is continuing. As previously mentioned, offenders are usually someone the child knows and may continue to see. They may endure not only the fear of disclosing but also the fear of being sexually abused again.

Child Sexual Abuse in Sports

It is suggested that between 2% and 8% of all athletes experience some form of sexual abuse.[16] Sexual abuse in sports and the failure to report incidents have received considerable

The Child Sexual Abuse Accommodation Syndrome[15]

The Child Sexual Abuse Accommodation Syndrome (CSAAS) is a syndrome that may account for a number of factors that prevent children from disclosing sexual abuse. They are as follows:

1. ***Secrecy*** The location of sexual abuse can be isolated or secluded; secrecy can also refer to the offender insisting on silence surrounding the abuse.

2. ***Helplessness*** Oftentimes, children are preyed upon by adults or individuals older than them who exude an air of power and authority, rendering them helpless to stop, avoid, or report the offender's actions.

3. ***Entrapment and accommodation*** Children may feel trapped in the situation because of not immediately disclosing the sexual abuse or due to the pre-existing relationship that they may have had with the offender. The children accommodate, or learn to accept, the abusive behavior by blaming themselves or believing that their actions somehow warrant the sexual abuse.

4. ***Delayed, conflicted, and unconvincing disclosure*** Delayed disclosures are loaded with limitations and questions regarding their accuracy. Even when children do immediately disclose, precautions are taken relating to them potentially being confused about a situation or circumstance. This can sometimes lead to charges being dropped and no penalty for the offender.

5. ***Retraction*** While children may retract their disclosures, there are also situations where due to the pressure and encouragement of adults, parents or law enforcement, children will take back their accusation. This is often done on "behalf of the child," so as not to put them through the trauma of a trial, or possibly because there does not exist enough evidence.

http://www.naasca.org/2011-Articles/060111-ChildSexualAbuseAccommodationSyndrome.htm

attention after being brought to light by the Jerry Sandusky scandal at Penn State. Despite extensive publicity, effective policies are still lacking in the sports community. Given the culture of some sports, athletes may "normalize" inappropriate behaviors and therefore not perceive the conduct (e.g., sexual abuse) by the coach as inappropriate.

The complexity of sport-related sexual abuse has increased because of the role of the offender. In this setting, the offender is frequently in a position of control and authority, making disclosure by the victim much more difficult. Disclosure in these instances can be delayed and may not occur until long after the child has left the sport or been far removed from the offender. For this reason, it is not uncommon for children being sexually abused by coaches to suffer over a long period of time.

Ignoring the Problem

In this environment, as well as other youth organization cultures, it is important that administrators understand and respect the seriousness of such crimes and the critical importance of reporting suspected incidents. Unfortunately, there are obstacles. The following is a quote published in a study of sexual abuse disclosures within sports organizations. The administrator is discussing a case that occurred within his organizations where several children eventually came forward making similar claims against the same offender.

> ***"What really helped in the case in my view was when the second [victimized athlete] came forward. If there had just been the first girl [the victim who filed the first complaint], a girl who is a bit emotionally unstable...Only girls who are kind of [emotionally] weak wouldn't realize when this happens that it is totally unacceptable. That girl who was a bit unstable at the time...I'm not sure she had the credibility to have him [name of the coach] formally accused and then found guilty."***[17]

On some level, there is an understandable hesitation on the part of many administrators to turn to law enforcement because they do not want to exaggerate a situation that may be harmless, harm the reputation of the accused, or harm the health and well-being of the child. However, those in charge must follow proper procedure once they receive a report regardless of the situation.

Reporting sexual abuse only *starts* at the initial disclosure. The quote above stresses the need for more effective procedures on how to investigate those claims. It also emphasizes the importance of taking all claims seriously, regardless of the circumstances. Additional children can be victimized by an offender who goes unpunished.

Another example of the problem of ignorance surrounding child sexual abuse is illustrated by the numerous e-mails between Penn State University officials about how to approach the allegations of child sexual abuse against Jerry Sandusky.

On June 8th, 1998, Gary Schultz, Senior Vice President for Finance and Business at Penn State, wrote the following to Athletic Director Tim Curley in an e-mail with the subject line "Jerry" when asked for an update:

> ***"Tim, I don't have an update at this point. Just before I left for vac[ation], Tom told me that the DPW [Department of Public Welfare] and Univ[ersity] Police services were planning to meet with him. I'll see if this has happened and get back to you."***[18]

This e-mail shows an ignorance about both the severity of the problem and the proper procedures to follow when allegations of child sexual abuse are made. Not only did the officials not know if or when the meeting with police had happened, but Schultz went on vacation in the middle of a significant time for investigating and protecting children who were being victimized.

On June 9th, Schultz informed Curley and two other officials, including the University President, of the following:

> ***"They met with Jerry on Monday and concluded that there was no criminal behavior and the matter was closed as an investigation. He was a little emotional and expressed concern as to how this might have adversely affected the child. I think the matter has been appropriately investigated and I hope it is now behind us."***[19]

On the contrary, this matter was not behind them. Sandusky continued to sexually abuse boys. These officials faced a similar problem but again failed to go through the proper reporting channels in 2001 when more allegations were made against him.

The report by a Special Investigative Council states that the investigation revealed "a striking lack of empathy for child abuse victims by the most senior leaders of the University" as well as "a lack of awareness of child abuse issues" and "a failure of the Board...by not having regular reporting procedures or committee structures in place to ensure disclosure to the Board of major risks to the University."[20]

A great deal of concern has arisen from the apparent lack of action and failure to properly report Sandusky's known offensive behavior to the appropriate authorities. Joe Paterno, Gary Schultz, and Tim Curley have been heavily criticized for their lack of response to the complaints. The timeline of Sandusky's of-

A Timeline of Offensive Behavior: The Jerry Sandusky Scandal at Penn State University[21]

1994: There were allegations of inappropriate behavior against Jerry Sandusky, the former defensive coordinator at Penn State, beginning as early as 1994.

1994-2011: Victims of Sandusky ranged in age from 7 to 13 years old.

1994-2011: Sandusky, like many perpetrators, began his sexual abuse with grooming such as touching, fondling, talking about inappropriate topics, and suggestive sexual talk. This escalated over time to full sexual encounters.

1994-2011: The victims were sexually abused in various locations including Sandusky's home, his vehicle, hotel rooms, and the Penn State football facilities.

1997: Sandusky founded the Second Mile, a charity that was specifically geared towards assisting "at-risk" youth boys, many of whom became his victims.

1998: A claim was made against Sandusky stating that Sandusky had showered with an 11-year-old boy. In a June 1998 interview with investigators from multiple agencies, Sandusky admitted to showering naked with the boy, admitted that he knew that it was wrong, and promised not to do it again, according to the Grand Jury report. The district attorney advised investigators that no charges be filed and the University police chief instructed that the case be closed.

1999: Sandusky retired, but was still given access to the facilities where he continued to carry out his sexual abuse of boys from the Second Mile charity organization.

2001: Athletic Director Tim Curley was notified after an eyewitness informed Joe Paterno, then head football coach at Penn State, that he saw Sandusky sexually abusing a boy.

2001: About a week later, Mr. Curley and Gary Schultz, senior vice president for finance and business, met with the eyewitness, then told

[Continued]

Sandusky that he could not bring any children from the Second Mile onto campus. Later, a Grand Jury said that Mr. Curley acknowledged that this ban was unenforceable. The university officials did not alert law enforcement.

2008: Despite the early suspicions and allegations dating back to 1994, the investigation into child sexual abuse by Jerry Sandusky did not begin until 2008.

2011: Sandusky was ultimately arrested on November 5, 2011 on charges of "sexually abusing eight boys over a 15 year period." He was found guilty on 45 counts of the total 48 counts against him. Sandusky admitted in an interview, "I have horsed around with kids. I have showered after workouts. I have hugged them."

2012: In June of 2012, Jerry Sandusky's son came forward accusing him of abuse.

Here are some of the disturbing accounts of the victims and persons involved in this case.

- The Tickle Monster
- "Who would believe kids?"
- In the basement, nobody can hear you scream.
- Creepy love letters
- "He told me that if I ever told anyone, I'd never see my family again."
- A skin-on-skin smacking sound
- Sandusky has "a heart of gold": how the school counselor reassured the young victim who finally found the courage to confide
- Raspberries blown on the tummy
- The crying janitor, who has seen too much.
- "It is just remarkable how many children one man can shower with."
- A young man, now shaken by the sight of chest hair.

fensive behavior highlights common grooming methods used, the failure to report, and victim trauma as a result of ignoring the problem.

Steps Towards Increasing Reports of CSA

Under-reporting can sometimes be attributed to the professionals who are responsible for reporting the suspected abuse. In order to combat the problem of under-reporting, teachers and individuals who work with children in various capacities should be trained in policies and procedures so that they

- Know how to identify possible sexual abuse
- Know what steps to take to report the suspicion to the appropriate person or agency

Organizations need to make their reporting policies clear and concise to anyone witnessing or suspecting child sexual abuse. Clear policies help to identify the appropriate channels of communication through which reports must be made. An organization may have pre-existing policies already in place but if an employee is confused about who the "appropriate authority" to report to is, or how exactly to report the abuse, they could become deterred from doing so for fear of doing it incorrectly or receiving backlash for not proceeding correctly.

Law enforcement should also establish policies to encourage reporting, including

- Emphasizing the criminal seriousness of such offenses
- Providing incentives to report
- Making reporting easier
- Working with schools about policies con-

cerning when to involve the police.[22]

It is important to note that individuals required to report sexual abuse can be legally culpable for not reporting it. In some instances, it is a felony offense to not report an incident when required by law.

See Appendix A and B for sample state statutes requiring mandatory reporting and the penalties for the failure to report child sexual abuse.

Characteristics of Offenders and Victims

There are a number of aspects of child sexual abuse and child/ offender relationships. They include:

- Offender characteristics and the subgroup of professional perpetrators
- Offenders' methods of grooming and maintaining an abusive relationship
- Common victim characteristics
- Victim Impact

Offender Characteristics

Offenders may have some similar attributes and grooming patterns, however, there is no profile, per se, of a typical abuser. There are no standard characteristics that are predicative of an offender of child sexual abuse. Hearing the word "profile" can turn into prejudice and assumption of guilt of certain persons. While there may be common traits, not everyone that has one of these traits (e.g.., not being married) is by any means automatically an abuser. Information may vary depending on the study being used, but what will follow is a general discussion of the grooming methods most commonly found among child sexual offenders who have been classified as extra-familial (i.e., unknown to the child or known to the child but not part of the child's family).

Within the group of extra-familial offenders is a subgroup commonly referred to as "professional perpetrators." Professional perpetrators use their working environment to prey upon children. This subgroup encompasses those offenders who use their employment at youth-serving organizations to get close to children for the purpose of committing acts of child sexual abuse.

Although there are a number of studies that have gathered data on the demographics of extra-familial child offenders, there is neither enough research nor sufficient sample sizes to identify conclusively the demographics of extra-familial offenders or "professional perpetrators." Keep in mind that research on this particular group of offenders is still relatively new and access to these offenders can be difficult. What is known is that extra-familial offenders, including *professional perpetrators*, tend to use similar "grooming" patterns and methods of maintaining the abusive relationship.

Grooming

Grooming is the process of how offenders make initial contact with the intended victims and the methods they use to develop a relationship with children in an attempt to normalize their behavior. It is a premeditated behavior intended to manipulate potential victims into complying with the sexual abuse.[23]

Grooming techniques can include

- Emotional coercion
- Physical force
- Taking the child away from their normal environment
- Seeing the child outside of the organization
- Giving the child a ride home
- Taking the child away overnight
- Testing reactions to sexual language/ materials
- Giving gifts, presents, or bribes
- Playing games
- Teaching the child a sport or a musical instrument
- Trying to become friends with the child
- Methodically and increasingly touching the child
- Bathing or dressing the child
- Using affection and making an emotional connection with the child
- Gaining the trust of the child's family to gain consistent and trusted access to the child

CAVEAT: Not all these behaviors are indicative of a person being an abuser. Teaching a child how to play an instrument is not, in most cases, a predatory behavior. It is when these behaviors are done with malicious intent to abuse that they become grooming patterns.

The following is a quote by an offender about his grooming methods:

> ***"Children are so trusting. A good way to approach is to ask the time. Seems innocent enough, but once you get them in conversation, it's hard for them to get away. If you look respectable, they figure you can't be a nasty stranger."***[24]

In this example, the offender begins by using the common grooming method of trying to become friends with the child. Asking the time of day seems harmless, but it can open the door for escalating behavior.

Maintaining the Abusive Relationship

Many offenders will continue to sexually abuse the same victim, sometimes for years after the initial contact. In order to maintain the abusive relationship, offenders use tactics such as

- Coercion
- Threatening force or harm
- Using guilt, shame, and blame

- Normalizing the behavior
- Using authority or power
- Using their employment and position working in close proximity to the child

When asked about methods for maintaining the abusive relationship, another abuse case offender stated that "secrecy and blame were my best weapons. Most kids worry that they are to blame for the abuse and that they should keep it a secret."[25] Guilt, shame, and blame are used as tools of coercion in order to build and maintain an air of secrecy surrounding the sexual abuse.

Environments for Abuse

Environment can play a significant role in whether offenders are able to commit abuse. Historically, childcare and youth-serving organizations created conditions where individuals, in positions of authority, were able to abuse their power. At times, emotional, physical, and sexual abuse were enabled by the indifferent collusion of or even the active support of the institutional management structures.[26]

Offenders will use various situations, both physical and non-physical, to abuse such as: preying upon parents who may entrust their child to someone they do not know well, initiating and taking advantage of circumstances that place the offender and child alone (one-on-one), or using physical features such as closed or un-monitored hallways, locked closets or rooms to commit abuse.

Later, this publication will discuss how to create both an organizational culture and physical environment which will aid in preventing child sexual abuse by professional perpetrators.

Common Victim Characteristics

Similar to their being no definitive "profile" of an offender, there is also no "profile" of a typical victim of child sexual abuse. However certain characteristics may make some children more vulnerable to abuse or to an offender. Jerry Sandusky targeted young boys in the Second Mile charity organization, which was geared towards at-risk children living in disadvantaged circumstances.

One method used to help understand victimization is to gather information directly from the individuals who sexually abuse children regarding how they choose their victims. This perspective is invaluable to future procedures and policies to prevent child sexual abuse. One offender commented, "You can spot the child who is unsure of himself and target him with compliments and positive attention."[27] Others placed importance on having a special relationship with the intended victim.

The offenders also stated that the child who was most vulnerable

- Had family problems
- Was alone
- Was curious
- Was pretty
- Was trusting
- Dressed "provocatively"
- Was young or small
- Was not confident/Had low self-esteem[28]

This information is useful because it is coming directly from the offenders themselves and may provide important insight into how victims are chosen. There are similarities in offender targeting strategies. For example, one offender commented on the benefit of the child's familial structure by stating, "Mothers are stressed, overworked and grateful for someone taking one of the children out for a while."[29] Because of family problems or the way the child's familial support structure was set up, the offender was able to gain one-on-one access to the child. Offenders will often try different tactics specifically to get the child alone.

Accessibility is a key victim characteristic.

Vulnerable Populations

Youth-serving organizations serve all children including those with specific needs or vulnerabilities. Offenders often target these children because they perceive them to be easy targets. Youth-serving organizations should be mindful of this risk and place no less importance or credibility on accusations made by children of vulnerable populations.

Some examples of vulnerable populations:

- Children with special needs
- Children who have experienced a recent trauma
- Children with low self esteem
- Poly-victimized children

Poly-Victimization

The term poly-victimization refers to individuals, in this case children, who have experienced multiple types of victimizations, such as emotional and physical abuse. A child who is a victim of poly-victimization is often at a greater risk of being victimized again.

For Parents:
Recognizing Possible Signs of Abuse

Parents should learn how to recognize the possible signs of sexual abuse. This list does not contain all potential signs, and a more complete list with age-specific signs can be found at ***Stop it Now***'s website http://www.stopitnow.org/warning_signs_child_behavior. It can be a single sign or any combination of the following:

- Destructive behavior
- Refusal to eat/change in eating habits
- Sudden mood swings
- Withdrawal
- Leaves hints or clues that they want to talk
- Has money, toys, or other gifts without reason
- Thinks negatively about their body
- Suddenly develops a refusal or discomfort with undressing
- Sexual promiscuity
- Bed wetting
- Abuse of drugs or alcohol
- Depression or anxiety
- Suicide attempts
- Fear of people
- Fear of closeness

Physical warning signs can include the following:

- Pain, discoloration, bleeding, or discharges in genitals, anus, or mouth
- Persistent or recurring pain during urination and bowel movements
- Wetting and soiling accidents unrelated to toilet training

Caveat: Having one or more of these signs does not conclusively indicate that your child is a victim. You should keep open lines of communication with your child to further clarify the causes of these symptoms.

**Victim Impact:
Lisa's Story**

Lisa was twelve years old when her family sent her to summer camp in New Hampshire.

Like most children going to camp, she was looking forward to spending part of the summer with other children her age, swimming, playing sports, and just plain hanging out.

Instead, Lisa "fell in love" with Mike, her twenty-five year-old camp counselor.

Over the course of that summer and the one following, Mike seduced Lisa and had sexual intercourse with her countless times. While it's no surprise that Lisa lost her virginity and a whole lot more to Mike, she thought she loved him and he her.

That was until they were having lunch one day during that second summer when she saw Mike's open wallet. It contained several photos of other young girls just like her.

She was devastated.

As it turns out, Mike was also a fifth grade teacher, but one with a particular preference for young girls.

Now in her late forties with no counseling along the way to treat her trauma, Lisa's life is **in disarray**. She suffers from severe substance abuse, an undiagnosed personality disorder, and is estranged from her family.

However, she still loves Mike, who died at the age of forty-five, and doesn't blame him.

After all, she gave him her virginity after she fell in love.

It is important to note that victim characteristics differ with regard to intra- and extra-familial child sexual abuse. Research has provided insight into who is most often a victim of abuse. For instance, research has found

- 20% of child sexual abuse victims are under the age of 8.[30]
- The average age of first abuse is 9.9 years for boys and 9.6 years for girls.[31]
- 73% of "professional perpetrators" were accused of sexually abusing only male children.[32]
- 81% of child sexual abuse incidents for all ages occur in one-perpetrator to one-child victim circumstances[33].
- 6 - 11 year old children are most likely (23%) to be abused in multi-victim circumstances.[34]

Victim Impact

The impact of child sexual abuse on its victims is a constant reminder of the importance of reducing the risk of child sexual abuse. Although there is clear agreement that sexual abuse is harmful for children, there is a lack of consensus on long-term consequences, what constitutes appropriate psychotherapy, and what public health policies should be developed to prevent sexual abuse.[35]

Effects of child sexual abuse may be obvious if reported immediately following the incident; however, estimates suggest that between 30% and 80% of victims purposefully do not disclose sexual abuse before adulthood.[36] Thus, the effects occurring over the span of years prior to disclosure may not initially be linked to the abuse. In addition, while short- and long-term effects of child sexual abuse are abundant, not all children who experience sexual abuse experience negative effects from it.

Although effects are not limited to mental health, at least 80% of 21-year-olds who were sexually abused as children met criteria for at least one psychological disorder.[37] Other effects are wide-ranging and a victim could experience none or a combination of many of the below effects.

- Post-traumatic stress disorder (PTSD)
- Depression
- Suicide
- Sexual promiscuity
- Poor academic performance
- Substance abuse
- Isolation
- Obesity or eating disorders
- Smoking
- Sleep difficulties
- Revictimization
- Homelessness
- Compromised immune system functioning
- Pregnancy
- Sexual, gynecological and reproductive concerns
- Other physiological disorders

All forms of child sexual abuse can also lead to criminal behavior by the victims. Studies show

For Parents:
What if My Child Discloses Abuse?

If your child discloses abuse to you

Don't panic or overreact to the information your child tells you.

Don't criticize your child or tell your child he/she misunderstood what happened.

Do respect your child's privacy and take your child to a place where the two of you can talk without interruptions or distraction.

Do reassure your child that he/she is not to blame for what happened. Tell him/her that you appreciate being told about the incident and will help to make sure that it won't happen again.

Do go with your child to law enforcement and report the abuse immediately.

Do consult your family doctor or other child abuse authority about the need for medical care or counseling for your child.

Adapted from the Boy Scouts of America Parent's Guide which can be found on their website at http://www.scouting.org/filestore/ypt/pdf/46-015.pdf.

that 14% of all men in prison in the United States and 36% of women in prison were sexually abused as children. Children who experience child sexual abuse and neglect are 59% more likely to be arrested as a juvenile, 28% more likely to be arrested as an adult, and 30% more likely to commit violent crime.[38]

Victim impact is not just about the effects themselves but also about the costs of those effects. A report published in 1996 by the Department of Justice, "estimated that rape and sexual abuse of children costs about $1.5 billion in medical expenses and $23 billion total annually to U.S. victims."[39] Another expense, in addition to mental health costs, includes teen pregnancy. Teen pregnancies associated with child sexual abuse cost about $2 billion annually. Sexually transmitted diseases that can be passed during the abuse cost about another $1.5 billion annually.

II. Guidelines for the Prevention of Child Sexual Abuse

This portion of the publication highlights specific components to the prevention of child sexual abuse within youth-serving organizations including appropriate pre-employment practices, the training of personnel, protocol on the interaction of personnel and youth participants, and the physical design elements of a facility that can act as a possible deterrent to potential abusers. Also illustrated are examples of policies already implemented by organizations that can act as guidelines for how to be proactive against child sexual abuse.

Preventing Victimization—An Overview

Youth-serving organizations are responsible for

- Providing staff and volunteer training
- Providing informative prevention programs
- Learning how to recognize signs or potential signs of child sexual abuse
- Following procedures and policies for reporting any suspicious behavior

Children should

- Be provided with programs to make them more aware of potential risks
- Be instructed on what to do if they suspect someone of trying to sexually abuse them
- Be taught to avoid risky locations where there is isolation or seclusion
- Be taught the common types of grooming patterns used by perpetrators
- Have open communication with their parents
- Be supported and feel that they can comfortably report behaviors that trouble them without being ridiculed, blamed, doubted, or dismissed

Parents should

- Be aware and knowledgeable about recognizing suspicious behaviors of potential offenders
- Have an open line of communication with their children about sexual abuse and actions that are not appropriate between children and adults
- Recognize the signs of sexual abuse
- Ask relevant questions of youth-serving organizations before placing their child in the care of a youth service

A. Pre-Employment Screening and Background Investigations

The first step in developing a program to reduce the risk that a youth-serving organization will hire a sex offender is to establish a comprehensive pre-employment screening program for all employees, volunteers, and contract employees who may have contact with the children being served by the organization.

While management for the YSO may not have direct control over the background checks conducted of contract employees (e.g., security personnel, cleaning staff, kitchen staff, etc.), specific requirements for those checks can be addressed in the contracts between the organization and contracting agency. It is important that management of a YSO establish minimal background check requirements for all staff, regardless of their employment relationship to the organization.

There is no guarantee that careful and considerate pre-employment screening will weed out all those unsuitable for a particular position. Unfortunately, there are a number of sex offenders who have no previous sexual offense history because they were never caught or because the accusations never amounted to charges or prosecution.

However, a reasonable effort to check the background and verify the information provided by the applicant will help reduce the likelihood that a child sex offender is hired to work with children.

Three Keys to a Successful Pre-Employment Screening Program

1. Do not rely on a single source of information about an applicant when making an employment decision.

Exceptions could include confirmed criminal convictions and/or proof that an applicant lied on the application form. However, a single source of information can be misleading. For example, if one reference is negative, it could just as easily reflect a personality conflict as it could a problem with the applicant. At least two, and preferably three references, may help to determine whether a pattern exists. The same problem can arise, for example, where a credit history report indicates financial difficulties that could be attributed to poor financial management, a recent divorce, or the loss of a job.

There are three points that employers should keep in mind about sources:

1. The information can be interpreted to reflect two or more different sets of facts.
2. The applicant should be given the opportunity to explain the negative information.
3. Employers should gather enough information from a number of sources before a decision is made about the applicant's employment.

2. Be consistent with the application of the screening program.

Screen for the position, not the person.

Screening for the position means that management has decided which positions within the organization require certain types of screening (e.g., criminal history, reference and education verification). When screening/ investigating an applicant's credentials, references, etc., be sure to screen all qualified applicants in the same manner, regardless of age, gender, race, ethnicity, etc. for that position. Inconsistent screening methods can easily lead to claims of discrimination by members of constitutionally protected classes of people.

3. Document your actions.

Documentation of communication, information obtained, sources, dates, and time is important to prove that the task was undertaken. For example, when a previous employer refuses to provide any information about a former employee (a common problem), the name of the person spoken with, title, information given — even if the source says "it's against company policy to give out any information"— and time and date of the call should be recorded. Many employers use a simple self-made form marked "references" for recording this information, then place it in the applicant's file.

If a problem with the applicant surfaces later in a claim for negligent hiring, discrimination or otherwise, the documented information may be helpful to resolve a dispute. It is often months or years later that such a problem surfaces.

The Elements of a Background Investigation

If the company decides to conduct background checks on its own, it is important to be aware of the applicable laws regarding methods of investigating an individual's background. An employer should use a variety of sources when screening potential employees. The resume provides a starting point for screening applicants in the hiring process. However, this tool may be more valuable if used in conjunction with other sources of information.

Some of the methods include:

- Employment Applications
- Employment History
- Personal and Professional References
- Interviews
- Criminal Records
- Education and Professional Licenses
- Training History
- Military Service History
- Credit Reports
- Driving Records
- Drug Tests

Although criminal history checks are a standard part of the screening process, they are not the end-all. In the case of background checks for YSO's, many child sex abusers do not have prior convictions for child sexual abuse. Combining criminal background checks with reference checks, motor vehicle checks, and interviews will go one step further to preventing potential abusers from gaining employment that allows access to children.

Some organizations have strict guidelines that any candidate with a previous history of

Sample Practices for Background Investigations

A. Every applicant is to provide all legally obtainable information that is relevant to the employment decision. (For example, the applicant should provide his or her full name, address, proof of a job related degree or professional license, driver's license number, etc.)

B. Applicants are to explain any material omissions in the educational, employment, or required personal history areas.

C. No applicant should be categorically rejected due to the existence of one or more characteristics considered to be unfavorable by the employer. The employer should strike a balance between the company's needs and fairness to the applicant. All relevant aspects of the applicant's background should be considered in making the employment decision.

D. Deliberate misrepresentations or omissions on applications, personnel forms, or in oral interviews may be considered disqualifying attributes by the employer. The employer should advise the applicant of this policy at the very beginning of the selection process.

E. The employer must perform the same level of background investigation of all qualified candidates being considered for a particular position to avoid discrimination claims.

F. Before an adverse employment decision is made, the employer should give the individual an opportunity to verify the information obtained from the background investigation.

child abuse will be automatically rejected. Other offenses found during the background process are left to the discretion of the company and whether they choose to hire the applicant. Policies should be implemented that indicate which offenses are deemed relevant to the position being filled and which are not. Company policies should comply with applicable federal and state law.

Legal Issues

There are several legal issues that employers need to consider. Every state has different laws and frequently, certain federal laws will also affect the way organizations can conduct background investigations. Remember, laws change often. This text is not meant to serve as a substitute for legal advice. The readers are advised to outline a pre-employment screening program for their company using this book as a guideline. Prior to implementing a program, have the proposed program reviewed by an attorney experienced in employment law.

The most common legal issues encountered in pre-employment screening programs include

- Negligent hiring liability
- Employee privacy rights
- Employment discrimination and violations of federal and local state statutes

Negligent Hiring Liability

Negligence in hiring must be understood before employers and their human resource managers can establish a loss prevention program to avoid it. Negligent hiring is defined as the failure of an employer to exercise reasonable care in selecting an applicant in <u>light of the risk created by the position to be filled</u>.

Negligent Hiring versus Traditional Employer Liability

Negligent hiring is easily distinguished from *traditional employer liability*. The difference is that traditional employer liability is actually vicarious or direct liability for the actions of employees while they are working on behalf of the employer. Negligent hiring is liability imposed for the employer's own negligence in the selection process.

In the traditional form of employer liability, the legal doctrine of *respondeat superior* operates on the principle that employers are responsible for the actions of their employees when tasks are performed on behalf of the employer and in the employer's general interests. If through the action of the employee a member of the public is injured, the employer can be held financially responsible.

However, this doctrine does have its limitations. If the employee committed a harmful act outside the scope of employment and not to the benefit of the employer, the company may not likely be held responsible. If the harmful conduct clearly falls outside the scope of employment, including acts that could not be reasonably anticipated by the employer, then the doctrine of *respondeat superior* does not apply and no recovery would be made against the employer. An example of an act falling outside the "scope of employment" could include assault, robbery, rape, or other crime.

Employers are not always exposed to liability just because they failed to check an applicant's background. Liability results when an adequate and legal investigation would have revealed a background logically connected to the wrongful conduct. For example, the failure to discover that an applicant was convicted of child molestation, when he is allowed to work in a day care center for children could result in liability should he subsequently molest a child at the center.

How much screening is enough to avoid liability?

Relying upon what other employers in similar circumstances do is not necessarily determinative of the appropriate effort required. The standard of care for adequate background investigations is constantly changing. Those steps that were considered reasonable twenty years ago may not be acceptable today. There are numerous cases where a defendant employer's attorney argued that back when the offending employee was hired, "No one else did those kinds of checks." Often, juries found the argument to be weak and without merit, resulting in a finding for the plaintiff.

Options for the Employer

Employment History

Checking an applicant's employment history allows the employer to verify information such as dates of employment, position or title, salary, job duties, and reasons for leaving provided on the job application. The employer may also research the applicant's ability to get along with others, quality of performance, interpersonal skills, and other qualities that may be relevant to job performance.

Frequently, information about an individual's prior employment can be difficult to obtain. Many employers are hesitant to provide information on former employees out of fear of a claim of defamation of character by the previous employer. Many employers have established company policies prohibiting the disclosure of any information regarding former employees to avoid being sued for defamation. Employers may also be sued for negligent misrepresentation for statements about the former employee that are not accurate or that may exaggerate the former employee's abilities.

Case Example:
Negligent Hiring and Negligent Recommendation

S.K. and F.C. v. XYZ Community Hospital

S.K. and F.C. were abused by John Doe when they were 13 and 15 years old, respectively. F.C. had initially met Doe when he was brought to XYZ Community Hospital for counseling at the age of seven, and although they only had a few sessions, Doe continued seeing the boy outside of the hospital. Additionally, he did not tell the boy or the boy's father that he had ceased working at the hospital. A few years later, Doe invited F.C. and his cousin, S.K., to his weekend home. S.K.'s mother called the XYZ Community Hospital to ask if it was a good idea. Doe's former employer was aware that he had left a former job because of allegations of exposing himself and molesting young children, but they did not reveal this to S.K.'s mother, or the fact that Doe did not work there anymore. Instead, they gave a positive recommendation. When the boys later disclosed abuse, the parents sued the hospital for, among other things, negligent hiring and negligent recommendation.

The court held in favor of the hospital for negligent hiring, because at the time of the abuse, Doe was not employed by the hospital and at the time of hiring there was no evidence that the hospital should have known that Doe was incompetent. However, the parents won the claim for negligence because when S.K.'s mother asked a specific question about Doe, the hospital was bound to offer advice in a non-negligent manner and exercise due care when giving recommendations.

An investigator may have greater success in conducting a background check with other employers, who may not normally disclose any information, by having the applicant sign a waiver authorizing the release of such information about the individual.

References Checks

Inadequate reference checks are a component of negligent hiring liability where the new employer fails to verify the background of the applicant through references.

There are two types of references generally, personal and professional. Personal references are usually those individuals familiar with the applicant who can provide basic information about the applicant's character (e.g., "nice person", "family man", "reliable woman", etc.). Personal references provided by the applicant are not likely to make negative statements due to some relationship between them and the applicant.

Personal references may be of limited value because it is highly unlikely that applicants are going to provide negative references about themselves. Again, as with most components of any background check, it is usually not wise to rely upon a single source of information in making the hiring decision.

Professional references are meant to include supervisors, managers, or even co-workers who are familiar with the applicant in their current or previous employment.

New employers can contact previous employers to verify such information as dates of employment, position(s) held, salary, responsibilities, quality of work, and other work-related attributes of the applicant that are related to the position to be filled.

One problem that is frequently encountered by those seeking information from previous employers is that many companies are so concerned that one of their employees may give out inaccurate information about the previous worker, that they have strict policies limiting information to verifying dates of employment and position held. Often, prior employers will give no information at all about an applicant's work history, for fear of being sued for slander, if the information is negative.

When contacting previous employers for professional references, written release statements signed by the applicant allowing for full disclosure can help to obtain the relevant information. Furthermore, some states provide protection to employers who release such information in good faith and when it is truthful, even if the information provided on the applicant is negative.

To obtain more information, the hiring employer can contact those individuals who had direct supervisory control over the applicant. Names can be obtained from the applicant during the interview. Typically, a more successful professional reference verification will result when these people are interviewed. Co-workers may also be a source of information either directly about the applicant and/or for the names of other employees familiar with the applicant.

Professional References

Professional references will generally be previous employers (the human resources department), immediate supervisors, or even co-workers who are more likely to be aware of the applicant's work history. Depending upon the nature of the position to be filled, the following types of information you may want to acquire.

- ***Dates of employment*** This should include what dates the employee worked for the previous employer, including day, month, and year.
- ***Positions held/titles*** Obtain details on all positions held by the applicant and the title for each position. Applicants have been known to misrepresent and/or exaggerate their titles and responsibilities.
- ***Tasks performed*** Titles can be very misleading. It is common knowledge that in some industries there are many people with the title "vice-president". The actual tasks performed will reveal greater detail.
- ***Disciplinary history/behavior problems*** A person's conduct on the job could be critical to hiring decisions.
- ***Reasons for leaving*** Again, applicants have been known to lie about why they left a previous employer. This question will allow for verification of information provided by the applicant.
- ***Whether they would rehire the applicant*** This is probably one of the more effective areas of inquiry. An employer who says no or refused to answer that question will signal a need to go further with the inquiry.
- ***The ability of the applicant to get along with co-workers*** Harmony in the workplace is essential for positive morale.
- ***General personality traits*** This is a difficult area to receive accurate, if any, information, but may be helpful in identifying traits that may be desirable for certain positions (i.e., outgoing personality for sales representatives). Note that personality tests, discussed in this text, may be helpful in obtaining this information.
- ***Work habits*** Asking about the thoroughness of the applicants' work and their work ethic can determine whether the applicants' work style is compatible with the organization.

- ***Quality of work*** Inquire as to the applicants' attention to detail, if they can complete a task the first time, the number of errors made, etc.

- ***Attendance and tardiness*** Determining how committed the employee is to the workplace may indicate how prompt they will be with completing projects.

- ***Promptness of work performed*** See if their work was usually completed on time and if the employee met time deadlines.

- ***Level of professionalism*** This is the applicants' demeanor or overall "presentation" of themselves. This issue deals with everything from appearance, grooming, grammar, use of inappropriate language or jokes, etc. It can be an indicator of how well they will represent the new employer.

- ***How well they dealt with the public*** Know how well the applicant dealt with the public, especially in the context of a service industry position.

- ***How well they handled a stressful situation*** Ask for a specific example or general impression. If the job they are applying for is going to be stressful, applicants should be able to handle that aspect of the position.

- ***Flexibility*** How well the applicant can handle changing priorities on a routine basis will be important to employers who have business environments that present such problems.

- ***Response to supervisors*** See how well applicants responded to requests by supervision, as well as how closely they needed to be supervised.

- ***Management style*** For the subordinate, ask what management style worked best for them. For the management applicants, ask what their style of management was like.

The Employment Application

An employment application can be used to check statements the applicant has made on his or her resume. An application should contain the following items:

- The applicant's full name, address, social security number, driver's license number, and any previous addresses or other names used in the past

- Education history, with names and addresses of schools attended including dates of attendance

- Employment dates, including name and address of employer, salary, and reason for leaving

- Military service

- Professional licenses, organizations, publications

- Professional references

- Criminal convictions (where allowed by state law)

- Certification that all information provided on the application and resume is correct (signature of applicant)

- A release statement authorizing the employer to verify information on the application

- A statement that any misrepresentation or omission will be grounds for dismissal whenever discovered

- A statement that employment is on an at-will basis and that neither the application nor any personnel forms are to be construed as an employment contract (where applicable and except for union positions)

Some employers may not choose to require an application form because applicants often provide resumes. However, resumes vary greatly in style and in content. And, since many applicants do not believe employers will check, they may "enhance" their resumes. An applicant's resume should not be substituted for an application or referred to instead of completing portions of the application. This policy makes the applicant accountable for information on signed applications.

Red Flags: What Should I Be Suspicious of on an Application?

What is a "red flag" on an application form? Anytime certain information provided or left off an application form strikes the employer as inconsistent or odd in the employer's experience, further inquiry can be made of the applicant during the interview for an explanation. The "red flag" item may simply be an oversight or could be an indication of an issue that may preclude the applicant from consideration for employment. Some "red flags" will be limited to the unique nature of the employer's business, but others are fairly common. Examples of common "red flags" include

- ***Unexplained gaps in employment*** Most individuals can account for their work or educational dates from high school through the present. But if an applicant leaves out several months or years of unaccounted time, then the employer should inquire where that person was and what they were doing. For example, the applicant may have been incarcerated for some criminal offense.
- ***Decline in salary history*** When a person's employment history indicates that they have received less compensation on each subsequent job and now is applying for a position that also pays less, an inquiry should follow. There are many good reasons why one's salary history has declined, such as a change in careers, desire to live in a different area of the country, etc. There are also negative reasons for declining wage histories, including incompetency, dishonesty, drug or alcohol abuse, etc.
- ***Dramatic career changes*** For the same reasons discussed under the declining salary history section, the employer should make inquiry of the applicant about the reasons for any dramatic career changes.
- ***Sections left blank*** Applicants may wish to avoid answering questions about their background due to a possible negative effect on their employment potential with the company.
- ***Unusual lengths of military service*** Most military discharges for non-career people occur after they have served a standard period of time in the military

Recommendation

If an employer is unable to obtain a reference from an applicant's previous employer, it should be documented. The investigator should make a record of the employer called, name of the person interviewed, the date and content of the conversation. The documented note may read: "I spoke with the Human Resources Manager, Mary K. Jones, who stated that due to company policy, she was unable to comment on the former employee's history with the company, except to confirm dates of employment and position held."

This type of documentation will demonstrate that the investigator attempted to obtain information on the applicant's past performance should a subsequent claim be made for negligent hiring of the applicant.

Supplemental Tools: The Diana Screen
An example of other options available

The Diana Screen is an example of a supplemental tool to use during the interview process. Organizations may want to consider utilizing these screens to help identify "red flags" that background screens would not be able to detect.

The Diana Screen is a "computer-based pre-hire/volunteer risk management screen that keeps children and teens safe from sexual abuse and sexual boundary violations. The Diana Screen asks a series of questions that identify applicants who fail to recognize sexual boundaries between adults and children."[40] More information about the Diana Screen can be found at http://dianascreen.com/

- Screens in the safest staff and volunteers to care for children and teens
- Screens out applicants who fail to recognize sexual boundaries
- Is easy to use and fast
- Is administered on a computer
- Is on a 4th grade reading level
- Is available in English and Spanish
- Returns immediate Pass/Fail results

Caveat: This test should not be used in place of standard background screening nor be considered 100% accurate.

service such as two, three, or four years. Career military members serve twenty or more years to obtain their retirement. However, there are a number of reasons why someone would spend a shorter time period in the service. Poor health, physical injury, misconduct, and budget cuts, are all examples that could be the cause for the unusual length of time.

- ***Reasons for leaving previous jobs***
  Applicants often leave this space blank, either because the reason is too long to write in the space provided or because the reason is not favorable to the applicant. Employees' ability to get along with others in the workplace, be productive and so forth, are all essential for the success of any business. Finding why an applicant left their last position may be helpful to determine their suitability for the position they are seeking.

The Interview

Personal interviews are useful in obtaining information not normally found in a resume or application, such as the applicant's general personality. The interview is also an opportunity to question the applicant about any inconsistencies found in the resume and application. A skilled interviewer may be able to screen out unqualified applicants. In order to maximize the amount of information obtained from an interview, *the applicant should do most of the talking*. The interviewer should use open ended questions and hypotheticals to help achieve this result.

Employers should have the applicant's application and resume on hand and question the applicant about the information.

Criminal History

The investigation of an applicant's criminal conviction history is essential to avoid hiring an individual whose criminal record indicates that they may pose a risk to children in the YSO, co-workers, or other individuals who they may come into contact with in the workplace. The employer's objective is to minimize the risk that a convicted criminal be employed in a position that represents a level of risk within the organization.

Research on criminal reoffending rates demonstrates that individuals with convictions for violent crimes and serious non-violent crimes (e.g., burglary, arson) possess a much greater propensity to engage in violent criminal activity in the future. Further, individuals convicted of serious non-violent crimes also possess similar propensities, such as the embezzler who continues to steal.[42]

The vast majority of negligent hiring cases brought against employers stem from the failure of the company to check an applicant's criminal history. To avoid hiring individuals unsuitable for a position because of their criminal past, an employer should undertake reasonable efforts to investigate all applicants being considered for employment in all risk-related positions.

Criminal history checks should be conducted on all volunteers and contract employees who may have contact with children in the YSO.

There are several components to the process of developing and implementing a criminal history screening program for new employees and other staff. The following steps are a suggested approach to establish an effective screening process.

Steps of an Effective Screening Process

Corporate Policy Statement

Managers need to establish an organizational position statement on the subject of crimi-

Questions to Consider Asking During the Interview Process

The CDC and the Staff Screening Tool Kit, 3rd edition, have suggested using specific questions during interviews to assess the threat of child sexual abuse posed by an applicant.[41]

- Why do you want this job?
- What type of supervisory situation do you prefer?
- How would you describe yourself?
- Was there a situation in which you were responsible for disciplining a child other than your own? How did you handle it?
- What age/sex of youth do you want to work with? How would you feel about working with a different age/sex?
- What about children makes you enjoy working with them?
- What other hobbies or activities do you enjoy? Inquire as to if the applicant has hobbies that include hanging out with children younger than themselves.
- What makes you a good candidate for working with youth?
- What would your friends or colleagues say about how you interact with youth?
- What is your favorite thing about children?
- Fill in the blank...I get angry when a child...?

What to Watch for During the Interview Process

1. Convictions, even if not directly related to child abuse
2. Rejections from other youth-serving organizations
3. Overly-cooperative/overly impatient of the process
4. Secretive about hobbies
5. Too much interest in particular age/sex of child
6. Difficulty describing appropriate versus inappropriate behavior or boundaries with children
7. Little involvement with other adults or adult relationships
8. Over-involvement in community child activities
9. Expresses over-interest in camping, hiking, overnights, or other situations that may present him/her with "alone time" with children
10. Refers to children as "pure" or "innocent"
11. Indicates a preference to work with a child that has a history of abuse

Not all of these behaviors automatically indicate that someone is an abuser. <u>However, do not be afraid of listening to your intuitive response.</u>

nal history checks that will indicate that the organization does check this data and the importance of such investigations. A policy statement should indicate very clearly that this program is important and is to be adhered to by managers as applied within the organization.

Risk Associated Positions

Management needs to determine which job positions represent a potential risk to others, should these employees be able to use their position to cause harm. Different job positions within a company or organization can pose a variety of risks by virtue of the work or tasks performed.

While there are certain categories of jobs that include inherent risks (e.g., working with children) most positions may not be that obvious. The employer must look at what exposures are created when the employee has "unsupervised access" to vulnerable people or dangerous objects.

"Unsupervised access" is the key in understanding how one determines whether or not the position sought to be filled is a high or low risk. Using this criterion, managers should write down each type of unsupervised activity/access that each position represents and ask themselves the following: If we hire a person with serious criminal conviction(s), especially for violent crime, are we placing our clientele at risk?

Risk Factors

Prior cases can be helpful to identify what factors constitute "risk" for a position in the place of employment. A common example of a position of "risk" is created by the <u>unsupervised access</u> to a variety of vulnerable individuals or circumstances creating an opportunity to cause harm. "Risk" is not a function of the employee's wages, job title, or skill set. Consider an employee's unsupervised access to the following as examples:

- Children
- Master keys
- Elderly persons
- Persons who are disabled
- Private homes
- Narcotics
- Patients—mental and/or physical illness
- Explosives
- Dangerous chemicals
- Weapons

The following is a representative list of risk factors related specifically to child sexual abuse within youth-serving organizations. Note that the emphasis is on "unsupervised" access to children in a variety of ways.

- Unsupervised contact with children
- Transportation of children
- Long term contact with children in live-in situation
- Extreme physical exertion in a remote setting with children
- Visit to children's homes
- Helping children change clothes, bathe, or with other personal activities
- Coaching sports in which physical contact between adult and child is routine
- Delivery of meals to children's homes

REMEMBER!

> ***The greater the risk, the more extensive of a background investigation is required.***

Criminal Offenses

Government agencies that deal with employment discrimination claims (EEOC and state level equivalents) generally require that the employer using criminal history data consider the relevance of specific convictions to the position being filled. In many instances, it is simple for an employer to identify the type of criminal offenses that are likely to preclude an applicant from employment. For example, no one would want to employ a convicted child molester to work in a youth serving organization or an embezzler to work in a bank. Unfortunately, this task can be more daunting when a prior conviction may seem irrelevant, given the nature of the position. The governing agencies discourage employers from eliminating all applicants because of a prior conviction.

Federal Legal Requirements

Equal Employment Opportunity Commission Guidelines—EEOC

Once a program is implemented, the EEOC Guideline criterion needs to be met to avoid inconsistencies in the handling of conviction data/information. The criteria for consideration of criminal convictions as a basis to preclude an applicant from employment include

1. Consideration of criminal convictions only, not just arrests where no conviction results.
2. Questions about an applicant's criminal history should be asked during the hiring process.

3. Criminal conviction information considered only when the company is ready to make a job offer (i.e., the candidate otherwise appears to be eligible or qualified for employment). This process will reduce the number of applicants who are screened for convictions.

4. Advise applicants that the conviction of a crime or crimes does not automatically preclude a person from employment.

5. If a criminal conviction is discovered, the company is to confirm the accuracy of the information with the candidate (i.e., to allow the candidate to explain the conviction and related information).

6. The company considers, on a case-by-case basis

    a. The nature and gravity of the offense(s)

    b. Length of time since the conviction(s)

    c. Circumstances of the job/position

    d. What the applicant has done with his/her life since the conviction(s)

Fair Credit Reporting Act (FCRA) Requirements

In addition to the requirements of the EEOC, the FCRA sets forth a number of requirements whenever an employer uses the services of a "consumer reporting agency" to obtain an applicant's criminal conviction history and generates a written report of such a history.

Thus, in any situation where the company uses a consumer agency report, the following FCRA requirements apply:

1. The Act applies whenever a consumer reporting agency is used to obtain reports of criminal convictions.

2. The applicant must give written permission to get the report (i.e., release form).

3. If an adverse decision (e.g., not to hire) is going to be made based on the report's contents, a copy of the report must be provided to the applicant.

4. A reasonable amount of time must be allowed the applicant to dispute the contents of the report <u>before</u> any adverse action is to be taken.

Written Procedures And Training

The policy and procedural steps should now be put into writing for all managers who are or will be in a position to hire new employees. Consistency in the manner in which the criminal history data is used in the employment decision-making process is critical to avoid arbitrary results and the potential for legal problems, including discrimination claims. All applicants who are being considered for the position should be treated the same with regard to the extensiveness of the background investigation.

Managers who are involved in the background investigative and hiring process should be trained on the company's procedures, including proper documentation of the actions taken.

Compliance With Local Laws

Employers should check with their local attorney to verify that the policy/procedures comply with state and local laws affecting the use of criminal history data. Not all states have the same rules and most have some laws requiring the employer to conduct criminal history screening of applicants for certain positions.

Proper Application Forms With Approved Questions

Frequently, employers will buy employment application forms from a local stationery store or printer without regard to whether the form is legal. Many states require these forms to contain specific language indicating the rights of the applicant and that the questions asked comply with the law. Before purchasing these forms, employers should check with their attorney to be sure that the form complies with local law.

Separate Forms With Signed Releases

In many states, the agency providing the criminal history data will require that the applicant sign a separate authorization form, allowing for the employer to obtain data about them. Use of these release forms may be essential to the lawful collection of this data.

Obtaining Criminal History Data And The Relevant States

Employers often assume that the only state that they should obtain criminal history data from is the one in which the business is located. This is not true. If the applicant has moved from or lived in another state, that state's records should also be checked. In general, the more recent the change, the more important it is to obtain that other state's information.

One way an employer can approach this problem is to determine the length of time in years that will be considered for the criminal history screening and look at all the states where the applicant has lived and worked during that period. If a seven year history is to be used, then all the states that the applicant has lived and worked for seven years should be checked.

Hiring The Applicant

During the time from when the applicant satisfies all other hiring criteria until when the criminal history information is received (sometimes there may be a delay), the applicant should only be offered the new position, contingent upon a satisfactory result from the criminal history investigation. The employer should consider providing additional supervision of the employee until the data is received to avoid "unsupervised access" to people or things that represent risk as discussed above.

Other Screening Options Available to Employers

Social Security Trace Reports

Verifying the information provided by the applicant concerning his or her identity, current and previous residences, and employment history is the starting point of any good investigation. Verification of the data provided by the applicant greatly reduces an individuals ability to hide criminal history or negative employment references.

By assessing national databases, the name (or names) associated with applicant's social security number are verified. Birth dates, previous addresses, and employment information are also cross referenced. If additional names or addresses are discovered, they can be included in the scope of the investigation.

Educational and Professional Licenses

Verifying the educational achievements and professional licenses held by an applicant is very important to ensure that the individual has the proper background needed for a particular position. Unfortunately, it is not unusual for people to inflate their credentials or simply lie about their qualifications.

Prior Training

When conducting the pre-employment screening, applicants' positions that require specialized training should produce some evidence of satisfactory completion of the program. Usually, the organization providing the training will issue a certificate of completion to the student. Employers should require the applicant to provide a photo copy of the certificate for each training program completed and required by the new position.

Unfortunately, applicants do misrepresent their qualifications and as such it would be unwise for an employer to simply take the word of an applicant that they have successfully completed the programs. There are numerous state and local laws that require individuals to be trained by an approved organization before they can be put to work.

Military Service

Investigating an applicant's military record allows employers to verify information the applicant provided on the application relative to military service. Employers may ask applicants to provide a copy of their honorable discharge certificate and/or other documentation of their military service.

Applicants may refer to some specialized training they received in the military service that is relevant to the position sought. For example, someone applying for a security officer's job may have attended military police school. In this instance, the employer should require the applicant to provide a copy of the certificate of training as proof that they attended and completed the program.

Credit Reports

Credit reports contain a person's financial history of credit card accounts, mortgages, personal and car loans, number of accounts current and/or past due, debt level, number of active accounts, and bankruptcies, if any.

Credit reports are also notorious for inaccurate and incomplete data. As such, consumers are often encouraged to check their reports regularly and have inaccurate information removed.

Credit reports also serve another significant purpose for employers. In addition to financial data contained in reports, employers may find information regarding previous addresses and previous employers. When cross-referenced with the applicant's resume and employment application form, the employer may discover that the individual worked someplace not listed on the application form. Consequently, the employer may discover another reference to contact. Often, an individual will avoid listing a previous employer who may have less than favorable comments about the applicant. Previous addresses also reveal the fact that the applicant lived or worked in a state not otherwise indicated on the resume or job applicant form.

Driving Records

Any company that employs individuals who will drive company vehicles, personal vehicles, or equipment on the company's behalf should obtain a copy of each person's driving record. A suspended license or poor driving record can expose a company to liability if the employee is irresponsible or negligent.

These records are readily available through the state's Department of Motor Vehicles. Information will include current convictions for traffic offenses along with the record suspensions, revocations, and expirations. The records should be obtained prior to hiring the individual to be reasonably sure that they do not have a negative driving history. Employers should watch out for serious repeat offenders and more than simple traffic violations, such as driving while intoxicated and at-fault accidents. It is also becoming more common for businesses to obtain an updated copy of the driving records each year.

Like any other negative background information on an employee/applicant, the employer should weigh the seriousness and frequency of violations and how recently the problem occurred. Someone with a poor record that is ten years old should not be scrutinized as heavily as someone with several recent violations.

Drug Screening

Public concern about drug use has led many employers to require job applicants to undergo testing for illegal drugs. Despite efforts by unions and other groups concerned with individual privacy rights, the U.S. Congress has not passed any laws forbidding drug testing. Many employers consider drug testing to be an effective technique to reduce the risk of workplace accidents, reduce absenteeism, minimize insurance costs, and provide a safe and hazard-free environment for the benefit of all employees and guests.

Drug screening, if done properly, can be an important component of an overall drug abuse prevention program. If it is fair and accurate it can have a strong deterrent effect on drug abuse in the workplace. When the applicants are aware of a company's drug screening policy, many employers discover an increase in quality applicants and that drug users will look for employment elsewhere.

Drug screening is generally conducted through urinalysis. Employers should always employ a professional and experienced drug testing company to help establish and implement the plan. Employers must be sure to screen all employees by position (job function), not by race, gender, etc. to avoid discrimination claims. Backup testing for validation is also necessary to minimize the risk of false positives, for the quality of the results depends on the quality of the testing procedure. A company drug screening program should be implemented in a consistent, fair, and equitable manner.

Sample YSO Background Screening Policies

Boy Scouts of America: Effective April 1, 2003, "all new adult volunteers in the traditional Scouting program will have a criminal background check. Social security numbers will be required for all new adult volunteers in the traditional program and all adult applicants must sign the Adult Application, giving informed consent to conduct a background check and no one may sign for another person."

Big Brother Big Sister: "To maximize the safety of the roughly 210,000 children it serves, Big Brothers Big Sisters advises it's nearly 370 local affiliates to screen would-be mentors carefully—even checking their Facebook pages. Then it requires the mentor, mentee and parent or guardian to meet at least once a month with a professional staff member."

AAU: "In 2010, under Florida Statutes, the following background screening requirements were imposed on independent sanctioning authorities defined as: all private, nongovernmental entities that organize, operate, or coordinate a youth athletic team in Florida, if the team includes one or more minors and is not affiliated with a private school as defined in section 1002.1. Under this law, independent sanctioning authorities, such as the AAU are directed as follows: (1) must conduct a background screening of each current and prospective athletic coach annually, and (2) no person shall be authorized by the independent sanctioning authority to act as an athletic coach after July 1, 2010, unless a background screening has been conducted and did not result in disqualification under the provisions of the law."

YMCA: "The YMCA requires background checks on all volunteers. Persons with a conviction relating to the safety or welfare of children or an offense on the child abuse and neglect registry, will not be allowed to volunteer. Those with any kind of felony conviction in the last five years will also be disqualified from volunteering, but will have the opportunity to appeal to the Executive Director."

Centers for Disease Control: In their publication, "Preventing Child Sexual Abuse Within Youth-Serving Organizations: Getting Started on Policies and Procedures," the Centers for Disease Control and Prevention suggested the following policies regarding background screening:

> ***Use background checks as one part of child sexual abuse prevention efforts. Using background checks alone may give your organization a false sense of security.***
>
> ***Save time and resources by delaying criminal background checks until the end of the screening and selection process. Applicants who do not make it through the written applications, personal interviews, and reference checks will not need a criminal background check.***
>
> ***Obtain permission from applicants before beginning a criminal background check.***
>
> ***Determine the type and level of check required for each applicant. Types of checks include name, fingerprint, sex offender registries, and social security number. Checks may be implemented at county, state, and national levels. Records are not always linked or comprehensive, so a thorough search may be needed to address concerns about an applicant.***
>
> ***Plan for the time and financial resources needed to conduct background checks.***
>
> ***Decide which offenses to examine in the background checks and which offenses will disqualify applicants. For child sexual abuse, absolute disqualifiers include violent behavior and child sexual abuse perpetration history.***
>
> ***Develop procedures to keep the results of criminal background checks confidential. Select a secure storage location and limit access to files.***
>
> ***Ensure that your organization's process for conducting criminal background checks is legally sound.***

B. Supervision of Staff and Volunteers—Policies and Procedures

Creating, adapting, and maintaining a Policies and Procedures Manual in youth-serving organizations is a component of providing safety and well-being to children as well as employees and volunteers. Many YSOs have already implemented and documented in their employee handbooks such things as "Code of Ethics, Standard Care Practices, and Guidelines for Conduct." The following section compiles multiple sources to offer a wide variety of policies to be taken as recommendations. Also, YSOs should check with their local state legislature to ensure that all state mandated policies are being followed.

Employee and Volunteer Training

Once employees have been hired, the next aspect of child sexual abuse prevention is training. Training should be provided to all employees and volunteers. It should also be offered to parents and other interested members of the community. Employees and volunteers will need a clear understanding of child sexual abuse, what the signs are, what red flags to look for, how to behave appropriately with children, how to report and to whom to report alleged abuse, and how to follow the policies and procedures set forth in employee manuals.

Training for parents and members of the community should focus on providing educational awareness of the frequency of child sexual abuse, grooming patterns used by abusers, warning signs of potential abuse in children, reporting suspected abuse, and what steps to take if a child discloses abuse.

Training can provide an environment that encourages prevention, recognition, and reporting of suspicious behavior with confidence that the incident will be taken seriously, confidentially, and be reported to the appropriate authorities.

Training is provided in a number of ways, including seminars and on-line tutorials. Most organizations require completion of training for all members and staff as well as re-certification annually, or at a time frequency designated by the organization.

Children should also be provided training and educational programs. One such example is the "Three Rs of Youth Protection" outlined by the BSA.

1. **Recognize** that anyone could be a child molester and be aware of situations that could lead to abuse.

Case Example:
Negligent Supervision/Failure to Report

Doe v. P-Co School

Doe found out that a teacher at his son's private school had sexually abused and molested his son for 11 years. Two years prior to the start of the teacher abusing Doe's son, the school had placed the teacher on probation after complaints of abuse from a different student's family. The school did not restrict his access to the children, and over the next 9 years, the teacher abused at least 28 students, including Doe's son. When another student accused the teacher of sexual assault, the school forced the teacher to resign, but still gave him a positive recommendation. Doe sued the school and two school officials and won. They knew about the abuse and as mandatory reporters, failed to report or curb the teacher's actions, allowing Doe's son to be abused.

2. **Resist** advances made by child molesters to avoid being abused.

3. **Report** any molestation or attempted molestation to parents or other trusted adults.

Another example of training for children is outlined by the *Boy Scouts of America: Child's Bill of Rights*, which gives children the following advice and training:

Trust your instincts or feelings.

Expect privacy.

Say no to unwanted touching or affection.

Say no to an adult's inappropriate demands and requests.

Withhold information that could jeopardize your safety.

Refuse gifts.

Be rude or unhelpful if the situation warrants.

Run, scream, and make a scene.

Physically fight off unwanted advances.

Ask for help.

CAVEAT: Children may not always be able to fight off unwanted advances or may not be able to recognize abusive behaviors or situations. Training should provide employees the knowledge to recognize inappropriate situations or the threat of such so that they can stop it before it happens or escalates; thus taking the burden off the children.

Sample YSO Training Policies

Boy Scouts of America: "(1) Every parent completing a youth membership form acknowledges awareness of the BSA's youth protection and affirms their intention to review the booklet, "How to Protect Your Children from Child Abuse: A Parent's Guide," which is included in every Cub Scout and Boy Scout handbook. (2) Parents and youth are required to review Youth Protection materials as an advancement requirement. (3) All adult volunteers are required to complete Youth Protection training every two years. The training is available online 24 hours a day, seven days a week. (4) Scouting empowers youth Personal Safety Awareness skills, including the "three Rs." (5) Youth protection information is communicated through videos and other written materials."

YMCA: "The YMCA is dedicated to providing a safe and healthy environment to the people we serve and to our employees. To promote this goal employees are required to attend and, where applicable, pass the following trainings; Cardiopulmonary Resuscitation (CPR), Child Abuse Prevention, Blood-Borne Pathogens, Employee Orientation and Customer Training. All trainings must be completed within sixty days from the employee's hire date."

Amateur Athletic Union: In an effort to help children and adults recognize the signs of abuse, the AAU in June 2012, implemented policies that will provide training for children and adults of the appropriate and inappropriate behaviors to be watchful of.

Staff, Coaches and Volunteers should receive training on the following:
"The definition of different types of child maltreatment, prevalence of child maltreatment in the United States, risk and protective factors for victimization and perpetration, common myths about child maltreatment, the requirements of the AAU Code of Conduct including the mandatory reporting requirement, all AAU Policies and Procedures related to Youth Protection, especially highlighting reporting requirements, handling disclosures, and personal conduct for employees and volunteers, case scenarios to have employees and staff identify higher risk situations vs. appropriate interactions between youth and employees/volunteers, immunity for reports made in good faith and for cause, and support available for the AAU regarding any valid youth protection issue."

Parents and Caregivers should receive training on the following:
"The definition of different types of child maltreatment, prevalence of child maltreatment in the United States, common myths about child maltreatment, warning signs for sexually inappropriate behavior, the

requirement of the AAU Code of Conduct including mandatory reporting responsibility, how to talk with their child about sexuality and youth protection, focusing on what to do if they are concerned for their safety of others and emphasizing they will not be in trouble for communicating about this, the caregiver's responsibility if he or she suspects child maltreatment and how to report this within the AAU context. Also, caregivers should be encouraged to contact law enforcement or child protective services immediately if they suspect child maltreatment, and a list of resources available outside of the AAU."

Children and Youth Athletes should receive training on the following: ***"Warning signs for inappropriate behavior, the requirements of the AAU Code of Conduct, the importance of reporting suspected child maltreatment or inappropriate conduct, the importance of telling youth that they should report any concerns to a trusted adult, and information about who is available within the AAU to who they can report concerns, and the importance of looking out for the safety of others and reporting violations of the AAU Youth Protection Code of Conduct."***

Adult/Child Interaction

Adult and child interaction policies are important to preventing child sexual abuse. They also help to reduce suspicious or inappropriate behavior between adults and children.

Adult and child interaction refers to how many adults are required to be present with a single child. These guidelines help limit the frequency of situations where potential child abusers are left alone with a child or children.

Suggested Considerations

The Centers for Disease Control suggest considering the following when determining adult to child ratios:

Age and developmental level of youth and employees/volunteers: If youth or employees/volunteers are young, you may need fewer youth per adult.

Risk of the activity: Does it involve a great deal of isolation from others?

Location of the activity: It is in a classroom that is easy to monitor or at a park, where it is easier to lose track of individuals?

http://www.cdc.gov/violenceprevention/pdf/PreventingChildSexualAbuse-a.pdf

Organizations should assess adult and child ratios based on their missions and nature of service. Organizations such as Big Brother Big Sister provide one-on-one mentoring between an adult and child as a regular part of their service. Consequently, necessary steps and precautions should be taken in these circumstances to ensure that abuse is being prevented and risk of abuse reduced. Each organization should also ensure that the adult to child ratios applies whenever possible.

Sample YSO Adult/Child Interactions Policies

Boy Scouts of America: In 1987, the Boy Scouts of America implemented a two-deep leadership policy. "One-on-one contact between adults and youth members is not permitted. In compliance with BSA's "two deep" leadership policy, two registered adult leaders or one registered adult leader and a parent of a participant, or other adult, one of whom must be 21 years of age or older, are required on all trips and outings. In situations requiring a personal conference, such as a Scoutmaster's conference, the meeting is to be conducted in view of other adults and youth. The chartered organization is responsible for ensuring that sufficient leadership is provided for all Scouting activities."

Amateur Athletic Union: In June of 2012, the Amateur Athletic Union announced that it would be banning all one-on-one interaction between adults and youth as part of it's newly adopted policies for prevention that had been recommended by the Youth Protection Task Force. The Task Force recommended that, "one-on-one interactions between adults and youth must only occur within sight of other adults and youth athletes. Whenever feasible, two adults should be present or, at a minimum, conversations should be held in full view of other adults. This protects both the youth athlete from abuse and the adults with whom they interact from false allegations. There are no exceptions to this rule, including for purposes of transportation of a youth athlete to or from an event or training activity or at any other free time."

Traveling, Group Outings, and Overnights

Another challenge to child sexual abuse prevention policies is the "special circumstances" where policies may not be easily followed or the environment may make it necessary to adopt different policies. Examples include The Boy Scouts of America, who provide youth with outdoor experiences such as hiking, camping, and overnights in the woods, and athletic teams where frequent traveling and overnight stays at hotels for tournaments and games are required. Organizations should maintain a focus on prevention in these situations and develop special protocols in a continued effort to prevent abuse and minimize the risk of potential abuse.

Sample Traveling, Outings, and Overnight Policies

Boy Scouts of America: In addition to mandating the two-deep leadership rule, the BSA also stresses the privacy of youth and adults. "Adult leaders must respect the privacy of members and protect their own privacy especially in situations such as changing clothes and taking showers at camp. The BSA strongly encourages councils to have separate shower and latrine facilities for females as well as separate facilities for youth. When separate facilities are not available, separate times for male and female and/or youth and adult showering should be scheduled and posted. No youth is permitted to sleep in the tent of an adult other than his or her own parent or guardian."

The following policies also apply:

No fewer than four individuals go on any backcountry expedition or campout.

Male and female leaders as well as male and female youth must have separate sleeping facilities.

Adults and youth of the same gender may occupy dormitory or single-room accommodations, provided there is a minimum of two adults and four youth.

A minimum of one of the adults is required to be trained in Youth Protection.

Adults must establish separation barriers or privacy zones such as a temporary blanket or a sheet wall in order to keep their sleeping area and dressing area separated from the youth area.

For basic orientation flights, the adult licensed pilot in control of the aircraft is sufficient for the flight, while two-deep leadership is maintained on the ground.

CDC: "Your organization should define and communicate it's on-site and off-site physical boundaries. Decide and communicate when and where your organization is responsible for the youth it serves. This is particularly important in a multi-organization facility and on field trips. Develop environmental policies for field trips and other off-site activities, such as how to handle off-site bathroom breaks and use of public transportation.

Your organization should define who is responsible for transporting youth to and from regular activities and special events such as field trips and overnight trips."

Amateur Athletic Union: Recommendations made to the AAU by the Youth Task Force include the following: "Given the nature of many AAU activities, clear policies regarding travel and supervision must be adopted, and there should be open dialogue about the inherent risk if a youth is traveling with a coach. In addition to travel for AAU competitions, AAU policies should address the role and limitations of employees and volunteers in providing local transportation to youth participants. If AAU staff or volunteers will be providing this transportation, the youth's parent or guardian must have signed a consent form. No consent form is necessary if the child travels with his or her own parent. However, should that parent be providing transportation for his or her child's teammates, those teammates would need to have signed consent forms. Even with permission to transport from a parent or guardian, there should be no one-on-one contact between AAU adults and youth athletes, whether during coaching, counseling, transportation, out-of-town travel, overnight sleeping, showering, changing, or using a restroom."

Contact Outside the Organization

Child sexual abuse prevention policies discussed thus far have focused mainly on areas of prevention within the organization and physically within the organization's facility or locations. External and outside contact also require clear protocol for contact between an employee, member, or volunteer and child outside of the normal working environment. This can be one of the more challenging prevention strategies because it places more responsibility on the child and parents to regulate external contact. Frequently, coaches, volunteers, teachers, or mentors are known to the child's family and may even be trusted friends who have a prior relationship with the family before working with the child.

Parents should take advantage of any training that can educate them on what to do in these situations.

Sample Policies for Contact Outside the Organization

CDC: "There are two types of out-of-program contact restrictions. The first type involves the contact of youth with employees/volunteers outside the context of the program. Your organization should limit contact between employees/volunteers and youth to organization-sanctioned activities and programs and/or to certain locations, such as activities within your organization's building. The second type is contact between youth and people not affiliated with your organization that occurs while youth are under the care of your organization. Develop a system for monitoring the comings and goings of all youth and adults who enter and leave your facility. This system might include procedures for signing in and out. Also, develop specific policies about interactions between youth and people not affiliated with your organization if it is located in a building that

Why Report Abuse?

- ***Reporting is the Right Thing to Do***—Protecting children from offenders is the right thing to do. Organizations are trusted to care and protect children. The needs of the children should be put above the organization.
- ***Reporting Stops Abuse***—By taking steps to report the abuse to proper law enforcement authorities, a youth-serving organization can assist in stopping the ongoing abuse.
- ***Reporting Connects Victims to Resources***—Many states have resources for victims of crime in general, and some have resources specifically set aside for victims of child sexual abuse. These resources include free or low cost counseling and health care.

houses more than just your program or if your organization's activities take place in public areas such as sports fields."

YMCA: "YMCA staff or volunteers will not initiate contact with or accept any supervisory responsibility with participant children outside approved YMCA activities, including babysitting or weekend trips, even if parental consent is obtained." The YMCA also prohibits contact outside the organization with a policy that states: "Under no circumstances should staff release children to anyone other than the authorized parent, guardian, or other adult authorized by the parent or guardian (written parent authorization on file with the YMCA)."

C. Reporting Sexual Abuse

Reporting policies play an important part in the prevention of child sexual abuse. Policies and procedures should clearly outline the steps to be taken by any individual, employee, or volunteer who suspects or witnesses abuse. Organizations should create policies and environments that encourage reporting suspected abuse, and there should be a process that will be taken after a report is made. Reporting should be confidential and should be taken seriously unless investigated and proved otherwise.

Creating a Culture of Prevention

Creating sound policies provides a framework for the creation of an anti-abuse culture. However, merely establishing policies and educating staff and youth is just the first step. An anti-abuse culture goes beyond mere compliance with reporting laws and cooperation with investigations. The anti-abuse culture prioritizes the well-being of children by creating an environment that encourages reporting suspected or known abuse.

One important component of an anti-abuse culture is creating a network of support. Organizations should build partnerships with local child protection groups, law enforcement, and child advocacy centers. This insures that when a report is made, the organization will be provided with assistance from law enforcement and Child Protective Services, and the alleged victim will be provided relevant resources and support as well.

Establishing a proactive approach to the prevention of child sexual abuse includes setting policies in place on how to properly report a known or suspected abuse incident, who is held accountable to report, and what the process is once a report is received. Developing an anti-abuse culture begins with an organization's leadership and should be reinforced by staff and volunteers who work for the organization and who strive to protect the children they serve.

Making a Report

All 50 states, as well as the District of Columbia and U.S. territories, have laws and policies that specify procedures for making reports of suspected child abuse, where the "ultimate purpose of the reporting system is to ensure the child's safety and well-being."[43] In all of these places, the initial report may be made orally to either the state's Child Protective Services (CPS) or its law enforcement agency. However, the process varies from state to state. For example, in 20 states, mandated reporters are required to submit a written report following the initial oral report. However, in 8 states plus the District of Columbia, a written report is only required if it is requested by whomever received the initial report.

All reporting persons are required to provide similar data in their reports in every state, including as much information available about the following:

Child's name, age, sex, and address/ present location

Names and addresses of child's parents, guardians, or other caregivers

Information about the conditions in child's home environment

Information about other children in the same environment

Nature and extent of child's injuries, including date of occurrence if possible

Name, age, and address of the person alleged to be responsible for the child's injuries

Any other information the reporter believes might be helpful or relevant

Important Point

The Child Welfare Information Gateway has compiled a list of state toll-free numbers for specific agencies designated to receive and investigate reports of suspected child abuse and neglect. It is accessible at https://www.childwelfare.gov/pubs/reslist/rl_dsp.cfm?rs_id=5&rate_chno=11-11172.

Most of these numbers allow for anonymous reports, but it is helpful to an investigation to know the identity of the reporter.

After a report is made, the agencies receiving the reports will follow a screening process that involves reviewing the report to determine if it meets the criteria for acceptance. For acceptance, the report must contain actions that meet the statutory definition of child abuse or neglect in the state. Reports that meet the criteria are screened in and accepted for investigation, usually by the state CPS agency and within 72 hours. If the child is believed to be in imminent danger, it should be initiated within 2 hours and no longer than 24 hours.

Professionals Required to Report Abuse[44]

Approximately 48 states designate individuals who are mandated by law to report child maltreatment of any kind. These individuals are typically found in positions that have direct contact with children and include

Social workers

Teachers and other school personnel

Physicians and other health-care workers

Mental health professionals

Child care providers

Medical examiners or coroners

Law enforcement officers

Some states also include film or photograph processors, substance abuse counselors, probation or parole officers, domestic violence workers, humane officers, and clergy on this list of mandated reporters. In 18 states, any person who suspects child abuse or neglect is required to report the incident and in New Jersey and Wyoming all individuals must report the abuse.[45]

The standard for when mandatory reporters need to make a report of suspected child sexual abuse varies by state. The threshold is usually when the reporter, in his or her official capacity, "*suspects* or *has reasons to believe*" that any sort of abuse or neglect has occurred. Another common standard used is "when the reporter has knowledge of, or observes a child being subjected to, conditions that would reasonably result in harm to the child."[46]

For State Examples of Mandatory Reporters, see Appendix 1.

Interviewing the Complainant

When management staff for a YSO is confronted with a complaint of an alleged child sexual assault, it is critical that the complainant (e.g., parent, child or both) be treated with respect and a high degree of professionalism. As awkward as it may be for the employee of the YSO to receive a complaint of an assault, it is a devastating experience for the victims and their families.

It is important that the employee of the YSO, who conducts the initial interview, be thorough in the questions asked and sensitive to the individual(s) reporting the incident. Suggested open-ended questions are listed below. However, it is not just what questions that need to be asked, it is equally important *how* the questions are asked.

There are a number of basic considerations that the interviewer should keep in mind during the interview process.

The Setting

The meeting with the child and/or parents should be conducted in a setting where the information can be obtained in private, such that other individuals (employees or otherwise) will not inadvertently overhear the conversation. Privacy is essential to protect the confidential nature of the information on behalf of both the accuser and the accused.

Complainant/Victim Behavior

Given the nature of child sexual abuse as a serious and disturbing crime, YSO staff should expect that the complainant will be very upset and as such, should be prepared to handle the interview process with this fact in mind.

Victims of crime often engage in a number of different behaviors that may include denial that such a horrendous incident could have occurred; the need to assign blame to others, including the YSO; and, of course, anger that will likely be directed at the interviewer.

To aid in the information gathering process and to help the complainant deal with the painful nature of their experience, the interviewer should consider using some basic interview techniques.

Non-Verbal Techniques

There are a number of simple non-verbal techniques that the interviewer can use to help keep the complainant at ease, given the circumstances, and not further inflame the situation.

Eye Contact – maintain normal eye contact. Do not look down or away like you are embarrassed, ashamed or do not believe the person.

Body Posture – try to stay in a relaxed, but professional posture. Do not sit with your arms crossed or use a clip board as a barrier between you and the reporting person.

Barriers – If possible, sit at a conference table or without a desk between you and the complainant. Make sure that you are all sitting at the same eye level (i.e., do not have the reporting person sit in a chair that is considerably lower than the interviewer's chair – this latter item creates the subtle impression of power/authority, which is not appropriate for these circumstances.)

Distance – Again, get out from behind the desk and be sensitive to how close or far away you are from the complainant. If you are too close (e.g., closer than 30 inches) it can make people uncomfortable. If you are too far away, it can convey an attitude of indifference.

Touching – Generally, the interviewer would not touch the complainant beyond a simple handshake. However, if the complainant happens to reach out and touch the interviewer (e.g., on the arm) for reassurance, it is important to not recoil and pull back. The effect of recoiling could be devastating to the individual.

Vocalization – The tone, volume, and speed of the questions should be such that the person providing the information will not feel rushed or get the impression that they are being interrogated. If the complainant starts to raise their voice and yell at the interviewer, it may be helpful to lower one's own voice, which can have the effect of causing the other person to lower their voice too.

Verbal Techniques

There are also a number of verbal techniques that may help reassure the complainant that their report will be taken seriously and that the appropriate actions will be taken by the YSO.

Active Listening – First, let the person tell you the facts before you start taking notes. Then, review the facts while taking notes, repeating the information for clarification as you understand them. For example, stating: "If I understand you correctly, this incident happened at around 3 o'clock this afternoon in the rear playground?"

Stating The Obvious – There are statements that may help reassure the complainant that the YSO will do what it can to help them. Comments such as, "we will be sure to conduct a thorough investigation of this matter right away", the proper law enforcement authorities will be contacted immediately", or "we will do whatever we can to help you through this process".

Personalized Statements – Statements such as: "I know how you must feel" and "I know that this is very difficult to deal with" may be helpful to convey a sense of empathy in a professional manner.

Asking Sex Questions – Direct questions about what exactly happened, where they were touched, when it occurred, how often, etc. must be asked with sensitivity and without embarrassment. The goal of the interview is to be thorough but not clinical or "business-like" sounding.

Other Considerations

- Let the reporting person/complainant tell their story fully and without interruption before asking a lot of questions.

- Do not assume that the local law enforcement agency knows how to handle a complaint of this nature or how to investigate the incident. Sometimes police officers become too clinical in their approach, often as a result of having dealt with a lot of criminal activity on their job.

- Remember: Be a good listener!

- All evidence (e.g., video footage) in possession of the YSO should be maintained and protected. Some perpetrators may attempt to destroy evidence once a report is made.

Sample Open-Ended Questions

1. Tell me everything that happened...

2. Can you tell me about who did this?...

3. And then what happened?...(this question can be used multiple times throughout the interview)

4 Tell me more about...(If the complainant discloses all activities during their day, you can use this question to focus on the actual event being alleged)

5. You said that____, can you tell me more about that...(This question can be used to get additional information)

6. When you said ____, did you mean that ____ (Use this to clarify details. This question can be a method of making sure you understood clearly what was being said)

7. Has this happened before or just one time?...

8. Where were you when this happened?...

9. Did this happen this morning or after lunch?

Creating a rapport with the complainant is important. Reassure them that they are doing the right thing by telling someone what happened. Remember that the age of the complainant can affect their ability to convey what happened. Older children may have an easier time answering open-ended questions and recalling specific events, whereas younger children may need to be asked more specific questions.

Be careful not to ask leading or suggestive questions. Let them tell their story.

Failure to Report Abuse[47]

Nearly every state and U.S. territory imposes penalties on mandatory reporters who knowingly and willfully fail to report suspected child abuse as required by law in that jurisdiction. These penalties vary by state. In 20 states, the District of Columbia, Guam, and the U.S. Virgin Islands, penalties for failing to report are specified in their reporting laws. Upon conviction in these jurisdictions, a mandatory reporter who failed to report can face jail time ranging from 30 days to 5 years, fines from $300 to $10,000, or a combination of both. Failure to report child sexual abuse by a mandatory reporter is classified as a misdemeanor in 38 states, but this charge can be increased depending on the circumstances.

Some examples:

In Florida, a mandatory reporter who fails to report can be charged with a felony.

In Illinois, second and subsequent violations of mandatory reporting are felonies.

In Arizona and Minnesota, misdemeanor charges of failure to report can be upgraded to felonies for failing

to report more serious situations.

In seven states, a mandatory reporter may be civilly liable for any damages caused by the failure to report.

To prevent malicious or intentional reporting of unfounded cases, many states also impose penalties against any person who files a report known to be false.

For State Examples of Penalties for Failure to Report and Penalties for False Reporting, see Appendix 2.

Sample Reporting Policies

Boy Scouts of America: "All persons involved in Scouting shall report to local authorities any good faith suspicion or belief that any child is or has been physically or sexually abused, physically or emotionally neglected, exposed to any form of violence or threat, exposed to any form of sexual exploitation including the possession, manufacture, or distribution of child pornography, online solicitation, enticement, or showing of obscene materials. No person may abdicate this reporting responsibility to any other person."

AAU: AAU requires all volunteers and staff to report any incidents of suspected child abuse to law enforcement and to officials of the AAU and related sports clubs.

Boys and Girls Club: "If an employee believes that any employee of the Club may be acting in violation of any such law or regulation the employee has a duty to report the perceived violation, preferably in writing, to Human Resources within 24 hours of the observation of such conduct." "All Club employees are required by law to report all suspected cases of child abuse. Child abuse is any act or omission or commission that

Case Example: Failure to Report

A.Y. v. Board of Education

After a boys' varsity basketball game, high school freshman A.Y., who helped report the statistics for the team, was waiting for a ride home when the coach asked her to help him put some basketballs away. He then engaged in sexual conduct with the girl, and the assault was eventually reported to authorities. It came to light that several years earlier, another student had reported sexual misconduct by the same coach to the principal. A.Y.'s parents sued the Board of Education and won because the principal, a mandated reporter, failed to report the child abuse to the proper authorities, allowing A.Y. to be abused years later.

For Parents: Reporting Sexual Abuse

A helpful link for what to know about reporting can be found on ***Stop It Now***'s website, http://www.stopitnow.org/faq_response_to_abuse. Other tips include

- Encourage and empower your children to discuss and have open communication with you.
- Stay calm if your child discloses abuse to you. Reassure him/her that they are not to blame for what has happened, that they did the right thing by telling you, and that you will help to make sure it never happens again.
- Be sure to know whom to forward the report. Some states notify Child Protective Services (CPS), while others report to law enforcement. In some instances, both agencies are involved.
- Be sure to bring your child immediately to a physician if he/she discloses abuse.
- As a member of the community, you should know who is considered to be a "mandated reporter" in the event that you have to report alleged, witnessed, or a suspicion of abuse.

endangers or impairs a child's physical or emotional health and development. The following are the steps taken for a child abuse case: (1) Inform a Management Staff person immediately, (2) The Unit Director or a Boys & Girls Club official appointed by him/her will interview the child to the extent necessary to confirm the suspicion of possible abuse or neglect, (3) The Unit Director or a Boys & Girls Club official appointed by him/her will contact Child Protective Services (C.P.S.) immediately to report the incident. All reports to C.P.S. are documented as to date, time, person(s) interviewed and outcome, and (4) a complete written report is submitted to C.P.S. within 36 hours of the allegation."

YMCA: According to the YMCA manual, the steps that will be taken in the event of a child sexual abuse report are as follows: (1) At the first report or allegation that child abuse has occurred, the employed staff person it has been reported to will notify the program director, who will then review the incident with the YMCA executive director or his or her designee. If the program director is not immediately available, this review by the supervisor cannot in any way deter reporting of child abuse by the mandated reporters. (2) The YMCA will make a report in accordance with relevant state or local child abuse reporting requirement and will cooperate to the extent of the law with any legal authority involved. (3) In the event that the reported incident involved a program volunteer, employed staff, or YMCA member, the executive director will immediately, without exception, suspend the volunteer or staff person from the YMCA until an investigation is complete. (4) The parents or legal guardian of the child or children involved in the alleged incident will be promptly notified with the directions of the relevant state or local agency. (5) Whether the incident or alleged offense takes place on or off YMCA premises, it will be considered job related due to the youth-involved nature of the YMCA. (6) Reinstatement of the program volunteer, employed staff person, or YMCA member will occur only after all allegations have been cleared to the satisfaction of the executive director or his or her designee.

D. Supervision—Physical Design of Facilities

There are two general components to the supervision of staff and volunteers at a YSO. The first, discussed previously, is the establishment of policies and procedures that are designed to regulate the interaction between children and adults.

This section of the publication addresses the other component to supervision, the design of the facilities and a variety of physical security measures available to YSOs.

In the 1980s the architectural profession developed a concept known as *Crime Prevention Through Environmental Design (CPTED).* The basic premise of CPTED is to design a facility—both the interior and exterior, in such a way that the ability to observe areas and define physical boundaries is maximized. Designing spaces that are open and visible through the facility ensures that individuals with a propensity to commit child sexual abuse do not feel comfortable pursuing their abhorrent behavior.

The YSO facility can be designed to minimize opportunities for offenders to be alone with children in spaces, that due to their design, provide cover for the adult.

Visibility improvement suggestions included "landscaping, clear lines of sight, secure areas, windows in doors, no closed door; policies, and bright lighting." However reasonable these approaches are, more steps must be taken to provide more concise and in-depth procedures to effectively institute each or some of these techniques. Prior to suggesting these facets to improving the environment and prohibiting child sexual abuse, researchers must study environmental design and analyze to what extent, if any, these techniques would or would not be useful to preventing child sexual abuse in youth organizations.

Organizations should realize that many of these design features rely on the already established facility. A number of youth organizations take up residence in older, brick buildings, which can pose a number of detrimental design flaws including a lack of sufficient lighting, isolation spots, closed or locked doors, hallways empty of supervision or staff, a lack of visibility into rooms or areas and restrooms that may be located in isolated areas. Older buildings also struggle with a "front desk" area that would enable supervision over who enters and exits the facility and their whereabouts when inside.

In environments and youth facilities that struggle with such physical environments, other policies and procedures should be implemented to compensate for the shortcomings. This would include extra staff to supervise children and in areas that may be isolated, perhaps installing CCTV cameras in isolated spots, making sure that children do not go to restrooms unescorted, and implementing such procedures as two-deep, where it is required that each child be with at least 2 adult supervisors at all times. Access control on entry and exit doors could be useful in combating difficult sight lines, so that all personnel and outside visitors must access the same front door and pass by a staff member who would act as a leading security system into the building.

Access Control

Other difficulties arise in youth organizations that are housed within other facilities such as YMCAs. These larger facilities may have a hard time efficiently keeping track of all people who are entering and exiting the facility and whether they are members. Locations within such facilities that are areas for children's activity or geared towards watching children should be designed for them. This might include a child sitting area with glass walls to allow parents to keep an eye on their child, restricting access to children to only those staff members who are allowed access, as well as providing a policy for restroom time.

Policies should also focus on the release of youth (a form of access control); meaning that staff should be sure not to release a youth to any individual who is not authorized to take the youth from the facility. If the parent or guardian of the youth is late picking up their child, organizations may want to implement a policy of having at least two staff members stay with the child until a guardian comes to pick him or her up. If the parent does not show up, policy should dictate what authorities should be notified.

Design Considerations

For facilities that have outdoor activity areas in addition to indoor areas, environmental design can be very useful. Landscaping using the natural environment (trees, shrubs, walkways, etc), works effectively to keep both those inside the area safe and within the boundaries, and deters those outside the area from coming in. Sufficient lighting should be used in outdoor areas that are accessed during evening hours. Features such as fences could also be substituted for natural boundaries.

The objective of CPTED is to create an environment where visibility is increased by employing the following methods where applicable and practical:

- Landscape designed to provide open spaces with no areas of concealment. Low growing shrubbery should be kept trimmed to a maximum of 3 feet high and tress with low growing branches (e.g., pine trees) should have their limbs removed for up to 6 or 7 feet from the ground.

- Clear lines of sight, unobstructed as much as practically possible (e.g., buildings will have some solid sections or walls due to their construction) so that staff can observe most areas throughout the facility.

- Storerooms, closets and other isolated areas should be kept locked.

- Hallways with alcoves should be kept brightly illuminated, with convex mirrors and/or closed-circuit television cameras (CCTV) utilized.

- The use of windows in all doors (except bathroom, which is discussed below) to reduce hiding areas.

- Install and maintain bright lighting throughout the facility on the interior and exterior. For national guidelines on recommended lighting levels, see data published by the Illumination Engineers Society of North America (IESNA), listed in the appendix of this publication.

- Bathroom facilities for children and staff/ volunteers should be separate with strict policies prohibiting children from using staff restrooms (except under exceptional circumstances).

- Bathrooms used by children should be designed (where feasible) to have the exterior doors removed or reduced in size, so that only the lower portion is in place to prevent total concealment of the child.

- Rooms used for children's activities should be designed to use glass panels, half walls, and convex mirrors.

- All exit doors not leading to playground areas should have exit alarms.

- Other measures for consideration include removal of curtains, drapes and blinds; removal of inside locks on closets and workrooms; and outdoor storage areas should be visible from the main building.

For examples of child care facility design and architects, visit the following websites:

1. Miller Design LLC
   www.millerdesignllc.com

2. Studio G Architects
   www.studio-g-architects.com

For Parents: Choosing a Youth Organization

In discussing the roles and responsibilities of children, parents, and youth-serving organizations, it is important to provide parents with the tools they will need in selecting a suitable youth organization. Before enrolling your child in a YSO, it is recommended to ask questions about how it prevents child sexual abuse. Here are some suggested questions to ask:

- What are your policies on child sexual abuse prevention?
- Does your organization require criminal background checks on all employees and volunteers?
- Does your organization require child abuse prevention training of all employees and volunteers?
- How often is this prevention training required? Is it offered annually?
- Are your employees and volunteers aware of state mandated reporting laws?
- How are allegations of abuse handled? Who is notified? Is it required that law enforcement be notified?
- Are there any other preventative methods used during the hiring process to eliminate the potential of hiring a threatening individual?
- What are your policies on staff supervision? How are they supervised?
- What are your policies for staff interaction with children? Does the organization use a rule like the Boy Scouts of America's "2 deep" policy?
- Could I take a tour of the facility? (To see if there are any isolation spots, open/locked doors, unwanted access spots, etc.)
- Does your facility have CCTVs and other physical security measures in place?
- What is your protocol for allowing access into the facility or facility area by individuals? In other words, are individuals who should not be in the facility denied access in some way? Is there a locked front door, key entry, and/or a front desk supervisor?
- What is the policy on who is allowed to pick up the child at the end of the day?
- Who should I tell if I suspect my child is being abused or if I see signs of abuse?
- Are there policies and procedures in writing that the parent can have a copy of?

Concluding Remarks: Where do we go from here?

After spending more than a year researching the data about child sexual abuse, in general, and reviewing numerous publications created by youth serving organizations and state and federal criminal justice agencies, we have concluded that there is much to be done to reduce the risk of child sexual abuse occurring within those organizations.

While many YSOs have undertaken a number of steps to keep children safe, there are many such organizations that have not faced the facts about the profound risks to children that exist every day.

At a minimum, the following issues need to be addressed by YSOs and a wide variety of governmental agencies and academic institutions.

Universal Definitions There is a clear need to standardize the various definitions of child sexual abuse to reduce the confusion about the different types of abuse and what penalties exist applicable to each type. Formulating an agreed-upon definition of child sexual abuse would allow for more sufficient research to be conducted and less confusion regarding statistics. By accurately knowing the scope of the problem, child sexual abuse can begin to be combated and the frequency reduced.

Perpetrator Types Law enforcement agencies, Child Protective Services, and academic researchers need to include specific details on the victim/perpetrator relationship in the process of receiving, documenting, or analyzing a report. Once reports are received by data collection agencies, the agencies should also include more thorough victim/perpetrator relationship categories. This would allow for better delineation of data between complete strangers and those professional perpetrators who utilize their employment to gain access to children for the purpose of abuse. At this time, the number of categories used when defining abuse does not adequately reflect the complexity of extra-familial relationships.

Single Data Source The federal government should establish one agency that is responsible for the collection of incident data about child sexual abuse and all state and local agencies should be mandated to report all such incidents annually to the federal agency. Currently, depending again on how child sexual abuse is defined in a particular state, either CPS or local law enforcement (or possibly both) will receive the report. This is a problem because law enforcement data is collected by the National Incident-Based Reporting System (NIBRS) and Child Protective Services data, which is volunteered, is collected by NCANDS. Thus, both data sets are only receiving reports of half of the incidents of CSA. In order for the research to be more complete, it would be more helpful to have one centralized system recording all reports of child sexual abuse so that all the data could be found in the same place.

Identify Responsible State Agencies Each state should clearly communicate to its citizens which state and local agencies have jurisdiction over investigation and prosecution of child sexual abuse offenders.

Consistent Policies There should be no exceptions to the policies and procedures of a youth-serving organization. A number of YSOs hire parents of children enrolled there or use them as volunteers. Other times, the children of current employees are hired. Although these individuals may be well known and trusted, they should not be exempt from the preexisting policies. YSOs should maintain the position that all employees and volunteers undergo the same screening process as any new employee without existing ties to the organization would. It is important to remember that those who sexually abuse children are most often trusted and known to the child. These policies should prevent any individual from slipping through the cracks. Similarly, individuals in positions of authority should not be allowed special circumstances. As was seen with the Sandusky case, even after allegations were made and Sandusky was told not to bring young boys into the athletic facilities, no one did anything to actually prevent him from doing so.

Proactive Approach The long-term prevention of child sexual abuse requires a proactive approach. As stressed by this publication, all YSOs should actively participate in the development and implementation of policies and procedures to combat the threat of CSA. Suggestions have been made on how to set up and improve the functioning of preventative tools such as background checks and screening, staff supervision, training, and reporting.

Youth organizations should consider the following in moving forward to prevent CSA.

- Follow examples. There are a number of YSOs who have already implemented prevention strategies. Use these as a guideline in setting up your own.

- Do not get overwhelmed. There are many prevention approaches. Do not feel that you have to implement them all. Recognize the limitations and needs of your organization and go from there.

- Be clear and concise. Policies and procedures must be clearly outlined for all employees. Lack of communication and understanding can lead to failure to protect a child.

- Continue to grow as an organization. Do not expect one prevention measure to solve all the problems. Review how the current policies are working and expand them where needed.

- Remember that the top priority is the protection and well-being of every child.

Notes

[1] Myers JEB, Berliner L, Briere J, Hendrix CT, Jenny C, Reid TA, editors. *The APSAC handbook of child maltreatment.* 2nd ed. Thousand Oaks (CA): Sage Publications; 2002. pp. 55.

[2] The National Center for Victims of Crime-Library/Document Viewer NCVC.org. Retrieved 2013-07-17

[3] Douglas, E. & Finkelhor, D. (2002). *Childhood sexual abuse fact sheet.* Crimes Against Children Research Center, University of New Hampshire.

[4] Centers for Disease Control and Prevention (2013, January 18). *Adverse childhood experiences (ACE) study: Data and statistics.* Retrieved from http://www.cdc.gov/nccdphp/ace/prevalence.htm.

[5] U.S. Department of Health and Human Services, Administration for Children and Families, Administration on Children, Youth and Families, Children's Bureau. (2012). *Child Maltreatment 2011.* Available from http://www.acf.hhs.gov/programs/cb/research-data-technology/statistics-research/child-maltreatment.

[6] Centers for Disease Control and Prevention (2013, January 18). *Adverse childhood experiences (ACE) study: Data and statistics.* Retrieved from http://www.cdc.gov/nccdphp/ace/prevalence.htm.

[7] Darkness to Light.

[8] Douglas, E. & Finkelhor, D. (2002). *Childhood sexual abuse fact sheet.* Crimes Against Children Research Center, University of New Hampshire.

[9] Kilpatrick, D., Saunders, B., & Smith, D. (2003). *Youth victimization: Prevalence and implications.* U.S. Department of Justice, National Institute of Justice Report.

[10] Bureau of Justice Statistics.

[11] Douglas, E. & Finkelhor, D. (2002). *Childhood sexual abuse fact sheet.* Crimes Against Children Research Center, University of New Hampshire.

[12] Darkness to Light.

[13] Boy Scouts of America. (2005). *How to protect your children from child abuse: A parent's guide.* pp.23. Retrieved from www.scouting.org/filestore/pdf/46-014.pdf.

[14] Snyder, H.N. (2000). *Sexual assault of young children as reported to law enforcement: Victim, incident, and offender characteristics.* Washington, DC: U.S. Department of Justice, Office of Justice Programs, Bureau of Justice Statistics.

[15] National Association of Adult Survivors of Child Abuse. (2009). *Child sexual abuse accommodation syndrome.* Retrieved April 3, 2013, from http://www.naasca.org/2011-Articles/060111-ChildSexAbuseAccommodationSyndrome.htm.

[16] Parent, S. (2011). Disclosure of sexual abuse in sport organizations: A case study. *Journal of Child Sexual Abuse*, 20, 322-337.

[17] Parent. 2011.

[18] Freeh Sporkin & Sullivan, LLP. (2012). *Report of the Special Investigative Counsel regarding the actions of the Pennsylvania State University related to the child sexual abuse committed by Gerald A. Sandusky.* Special Investigations Task Force, The Pennsylvania State University's Board of Trustees, Pennsylvania State University.

[19] Freeh Sporkin & Sullivan, LLP, Exhibit 5F-H.

[20] Freeh Sporkin & Sullivan, LLP, pp. 16.

[21] Lopresti, M. (2012, June 23). Scarred kids can't leave Jerry Sandusky case behind. *USA Today*. Retrieved from http://usatoday30.usatoday.com/sports/columnist/lopresti/story/2012-06-22/jerry-sandusky-guilty-children-scarred/55769946/1

[22] Finkelhor, D., & Ormrod, R. (2001). Factors in the underreporting of crimes against juveniles. *Child Maltreatment, 6(3)*, pp. 219.

[23] American Psychiatric Association. (2000). *Diagnostic and statistical manual of mental disorders* (4th ed., text rev.). doi:10.1176/appi.books.9780890423349.

[24] Elliott, M. (1995). "Child Sexual Abuse Prevention: What Offenders Tell Us." *Child Abuse & Neglect, Vol. 19(5)*, pp. 579-594.

[25] Elliot, 1995.

[26] Sullivan, J., & Beech, A. (2002). Professional perpetrators: Sex offenders who use their employment to target and sexually abuse the children with whom they work. *Child Abuse Review, 11*, pp.161.

[27] Elliot, 1995.

[28] Elliot, 1995.

[29] Elliot, 1995.

[30] Darkness to Light.

[31] The National Resource Center on Child Sexual Abuse. *The incidence and prevalence of child sexual abuse*, Hunstsville: NRCCSA, 1994.

[32] Sullivan, J., & Beech, A. (2004). A comparative study of demographic data relating to intra-and extra-familial child sexual abusers and professional perpetrators. *Journal of Sexual Aggression, 10(1)*, 39-50.

[33] Snyder, 2000

[34] Snyder, 2000

[35] Johnson, R. (2008). Advances in understanding and treating child sexual abuse: Implications for research and policy. *Family & Community Health, 31(1S)*, pp. S24.

[36] Arata, C.M. (1998). To tell or not to tell: Current functioning of child sexual abuse survivors who disclosed their victimization. *Child Maltreatment, 3(1)*, pp. 63-71; Lawson & Chaffin, 1992, Paine & Hansen, 2002, Smith et al 2000.

[37] US Department of Health and Human Services, 2006.

[38] Child Welfare Information Gateway (1999). *Prior abuse reported by inmates and probationers.* Washington, DC: U.S. Department of Health and Human Services, Children's Bureau.

[39] U.S. Department of Justice (1996). The extent and costs of crime victimization: A new look. [On-line] Washington, D.C.: Government Publications. Available at http://www.ncjrs.org/pdffiles/victcost.pdf

[40] http://www.dianascreen.com/about-us/

[41] http://www.cdc.gov/violenceprevention/pdf/PreventingChildSexualAbuse-a.pdf
http://www.nationalserviceresources.org/files/r3300-staff-screening-tool-kit.pdf

[42] Langan, P. & Levin, D. (2002). *Recidivism of prisoners released in 1994.* US Department Of Justice, Office of Justice Programs
Durose, M., Cooper, A., & Snyder, H. (2014). *Recidivism of prisoners released in 30 states in 2005: Patterns from 2005 to 2010.* US Department of Justice, Bureau of Justice Statistics.

[43] Child Welfare Information Gateway. (2013). *Making and Screening Reports of Child Abuse and Neglect.* Washington, DC: U.S. Department of Health and Human Services, Children's Bureau, pp. 3.

[44] Child Welfare Information Gateway. (2012). *Mandatory reporters of child abuse and neglect.* Washington, DC: U.S. Department of Health and Human Services, Children's Bureau.

[45] Child Welfare Information Gateway. (2012). *Mandatory reporters of child abuse and neglect.* Washington, DC: U.S. Department of Health and Human Services, Children's Bureau.

[46] Child Welfare Information Gateway. (2012). *Mandatory reporters of child abuse and neglect.* Washington, DC: U.S. Department of Health and Human Services, Children's Bureau.

[47] Child Welfare Information Gateway. (2012). *Penalties for failure to report and false reporting of child abuse and neglect.* Washington, DC: U.S. Department of Health and Human Services, Children's Bureau.

Appendix 1: State Examples of Mandatory Reporters

California

Professionals Required to Report Penal Code § 11165.7

Mandated reporters include any of the following:

- Teachers, teacher's aides, administrators, and classified employees of any public or private school
- Administrators or employees of day camps, youth centers, or youth recreation programs
- Employees of a county office of education or the State Department of Education
- Licensees, administrators, or employees of licensed community care or child daycare facilities
- Head Start program teachers
- Workers or evaluators employed by a licensing agency
- Public assistance workers
- Foster parents, group home personnel, and personnel of residential care facilities
- Social workers, probation officers, and parole officers
- Employees of school district police or security departments
- Administrators, presenters, or counselors for child abuse prevention programs
- District attorney investigators, inspectors, or local child support agency caseworkers
- Peace officers and firefighters, except for volunteer firefighters
- Physicians, surgeons, psychiatrists, psychologists, dentists, residents, interns, podiatrists, chiropractors, licensed nurses, dental hygienists, optometrists, marriage, family, and child counselors, and clinical social workers
- Emergency medical technicians and paramedics
- Psychological assistants
- Marriage, family, and child therapist trainees and interns
- State or county public health employees who treat minors for venereal diseases or other conditions
- Coroners and medical examiners
- Commercial film and photographic print processors
- Child visitation monitors
- Animal control or humane society officers
- Clergy members and custodians of records of clergy members
- Employees of police departments, county sheriff's departments, county probation departments, or county welfare departments
- Employees or volunteers of a Court-Appointed Special Advocate program
- Individuals providing services to minor children
- Alcohol and drug counselors

Reporting by Other Persons
Penal Code § 11166

Any other person who reasonably suspects that a child is a victim of abuse or neglect may report.

For the purposes of this section, 'any other person' includes a mandated reporter who acts in his or her private capacity and not in his or her professional capacity or within the scope of his or her employment.

Florida

Professionals Required to Report
Ann. Stat. § 39.201

The following persons are mandated reporters:

- Physicians, osteopaths, medical examiners, chiropractors, nurses, or hospital personnel
- Other health or mental health professionals
- Practitioners who rely solely on spiritual means for healing
- Teachers or other school officials or personnel
- Social workers, daycare center workers, or other professional child care, foster care, residential, or institutional workers
- Law enforcement officers or judges

Reporting by Other Persons
Ann. Stat. § 39.201

Any person who knows or has reasonable cause to suspect that a child is abused, abandoned, or neglected shall report.

Illinois

Professionals Required to Report
Comp. Stat. Ch. 325, § 5/4; Ch. 720, § 5/11-20.2

The following persons are required to report:

- Physicians, residents, interns, hospital administrators and personnel, surgeons, dentists, dental hygienists, osteopaths, chiropractors, podiatrists, physician assistants, or substance abuse treatment personnel
- Funeral home directors or employees, coroners, or medical examiners
- Emergency medical technicians, acupuncturists, or crisis line or hotline personnel
- School administrators and employees, educational advocates, or truant officers
- Members of a school board or the Chicago Board of Education
- Members of the governing body of a private school
- Social workers, social services administrators, or domestic violence program personnel
- Nurses, genetic counselors, respiratory care practitioners, advanced practice nurses, home health aides, directors or staff assistants of nursery schools or child care centers, or recreational program or facility personnel
- Law enforcement officers or probation officers
- Licensed professional counselors, psychologists, or psychiatrists
- Field personnel of the Department of Healthcare and Family Services, Juvenile Justice, Public Health, Human Services, Corrections, Human Rights, or Children and Family Services
- Supervisors and administrators of general assistance under the Illinois Public Aid Code
- Animal control officers or Department of Agriculture Bureau of Animal Health and

Welfare field investigators
- Foster parents, homemakers, or child care workers
- Members of the clergy
- Commercial film and photographic print processors or computer technicians

Reporting by Other Persons
Comp. Stat. Ch. 325, § 5/4

Any other person who has reasonable cause to believe that a child is abused or neglected may report.

Massachusetts

Professionals Required to Report
Gen. Laws Ch. 119, § 21

Mandatory reporters include:

- Physicians, medical interns, hospital personnel, medical examiners, psychologists, emergency medical technicians, dentists, nurses, chiropractors, podiatrists, optometrists, osteopaths, allied mental health and human services professionals, drug and alcoholism counselors, psychiatrists, or clinical social workers
- Public or private schoolteachers, educational administrators, guidance or family counselors, or child care workers
- Persons paid to care for or work with a child in any public or private facility, home, or program that provides child care or residential services to children
- Persons who provide the services of child care resource and referral agencies, voucher management agencies, family child care systems, or child care food programs
- Licensors of the Department of Early Education and Care or school attendance officers
- Probation officers, clerk-magistrates of a district court, parole officers, social workers, foster parents, firefighters, or police officers
- Priests, rabbis, clergy members, ordained or licensed ministers, leaders of any church or religious body, or accredited Christian Science practitioners
- Persons performing official duties on behalf of a church or religious body that are recognized as the duties of a priest, rabbi, clergy, ordained or licensed minister, leader of any church or religious body, accredited Christian Science practitioner
- Persons employed by a church or religious body to supervise, educate, coach, train or counsel a child on a regular basis
- Persons in charge of a medical or other public or private institution, school, or facility or that person's designated agent
- The child advocate

Reporting by Other Persons
Gen. Laws Ch. 119, § 51A

Any other person who has reasonable cause to believe that a child is suffering from or has died as a result of abuse or neglect may file a report.

New York

Professionals Required to Report
Soc. Serv. Law § 413

The following persons and officials are required to report:

- Physicians, physician assistants, surgeons, medical examiners, coroners, dentists, dental hygienists, osteopaths, optometrists, chiropractors, podiatrists, residents, interns, psychologists, registered nurses, social workers, or emergency medical technicians

- Licensed creative arts therapists, marriage and family therapists, mental health counselors, or psychoanalysts
- Hospital personnel or Christian Science practitioners
- School officials, including but not limited to, teachers, guidance counselors, school psychologists, school social workers, school nurses, or administrators
- Social services workers, daycare center workers, providers of family or group family daycare, or employees or volunteers in a residential care facility or any other child care or foster care worker
- Mental health professionals, substance abuse counselors, alcoholism counselors, or all persons credentialed by the Office of Alcoholism and Substance Abuse Services
- Peace officers, police officers, district attorneys or assistant district attorneys, investigators employed in the office of a district attorney, or other law enforcement officials

Reporting by Other Persons
Soc. Serv. Law § 414

Any other person who has reasonable cause to suspect that a child is abused or maltreated may report.

Texas

Professionals Required to Report
Fam. Code § 261.101

Persons required to report include:

- A professional, for purposes of the reporting laws, who is licensed or certified by the State or who is an employee of a facility licensed, certified, or operated by the State and who, in the normal course of official duties or duties for which a license or certification is required, has direct contact with children.
- Professionals include:
    - Teachers or daycare employees
    - Nurses, doctors, or employees of a clinic or health-care facility that provides reproductive services
    - Juvenile probation officers or juvenile detention or correctional officers

Reporting by Other Persons
Fam. Code § 261.101

A person who has cause to believe that a child has been adversely affected by abuse or neglect shall immediately make a report.

Appendix 2: State Examples of Penalties for Failure to Report and False Reporting

California

Failure to Report
Penal Code §§ 11166(c); 11166.01

Any mandated reporter who fails to report an incident of known or reasonably suspected child abuse or neglect is guilty of a misdemeanor punishable by up to 6 months in a county jail, by a fine of $1,000, or both. If a mandated reporter intentionally conceals his or her failure to report an incident known by the mandated reporter to be abuse or severe neglect, the failure to report is a continuing offense until an agency specified in § 11165.9 discovers the offense.

Any supervisor or administrator who violates § 11166(1) [that prohibits impeding others from making a report], shall be punished by no more than 6 months in a county jail, by a fine of no more than $1,000, or both.

Any mandated reporter who willfully fails to report abuse or neglect, or any person who impedes or inhibits a report of abuse or neglect, where that abuse or neglect results in death or great bodily injury, shall be punished by no more than 1 year in a county jail, by a fine of no more than $5,000, or both.

False Reporting
Penal Code § 11172(a)

Any person reporting a known or suspected instance of child abuse or neglect shall not incur civil or criminal liability as a result of any report unless it can be proven that a false report was made and the person knew that the report was false or was made with reckless disregard of the truth or falsity of the report.

Any person who makes a report of child abuse or neglect known to be false or with reckless disregard of the truth or falsity of the report is liable for any damages caused.

Florida

Failure to Report
Ann. Stat. § 39.205(1)-(4)

A person who is required to report known or suspected child abuse and who knowingly and willfully fails to do so, or who knowingly and willfully prevents another person from doing so, commits a felony of the third degree, punishable as provided in §§ 775.082, 775.083, or 775.084. Upon conviction, the person may be:

- Imprisoned for a term not to exceed 5 years
- Fined $5,000

Unless the court finds that the person is a victim of domestic violence or that other mitigating circumstances exist, a person who is age 18 or older and lives in the same house or living unit as a child who is known or suspected to be a victim of child abuse, and knowingly and willfully fails to report the child abuse, commits a felony of the third degree.

Any Florida College System institution, State university, or nonpublic college, university, or school, whose administrators knowingly and willfully, upon receiving information from faculty, staff, or other institution employees, fail to report known or suspected child abuse, abandonment, or neglect committed on the property of the university, college, or school, or during an event or function sponsored by the university, college, or school, or who knowingly and willfully prevent another person from doing so, shall be subject to fines of $1 million for each such failure.

Any Florida College System institution, State university, or nonpublic college, university, or school, whose law enforcement agency fails to report known or suspected child abuse, abandonment, or neglect committed on the property of the university, college, or school, or during an event or function sponsored by the university, college, or school, shall be subject to fines of $1 million for each such failure.

False Reporting
Ann. Stat. §§ 39.205(9); 39.206(1)

A person who knowingly and willfully makes a false report of child abuse, abandonment, or neglect, or who advises another to make a false report, is guilty of a felony of the third degree. Upon conviction, the person may be:

- Imprisoned for a term not to exceed 5 years
- Fined $5,000

In addition to any other penalty authorized by this section or other law, the Department of Children and Family Services may impose a fine, not to exceed $10,000 for each violation, upon a person who knowingly and willfully makes a false report of abuse, abandonment, or neglect of a child, or a person who counsels another to make a false report.

Illinois

Failure to Report
Comp. Stat. Ch. 325, §§ 5/4.02; 5/4

Any physician who willfully fails to report suspected child abuse or neglect shall be referred to the Illinois State Medical Disciplinary Board for action in accordance with the Medical Practice Act of 1987. Any dentist or dental hygienist who willfully fails to report suspected child abuse or neglect shall be referred to the Department of Professional Regulation for action in accordance with the Illinois Dental Practice Act.

Any mandatory reporter who willfully fails to report suspected child abuse or neglect shall be guilty of a Class A misdemeanor for a first violation and a Class 4 felony for a second or subsequent violation.

Any person who knowingly and willfully violates any provision of this Section is guilty of a Class A misdemeanor for a first violation and a Class 4 felony for a second or subsequent violation.

If the person acted as part of a plan or scheme having as its object the prevention of discovery of an abused or neglected child by lawful authorities for the purpose of protecting or insulating any person or entity from arrest or prosecution, the person is guilty of a Class 4 felony for a first offense and a Class 3 felony for a second or subsequent offense (regardless of whether the second or subsequent offense involves any of the same facts or persons as the first or other prior offense).

False Reporting
Comp. Stat. Ch. 325, § 5/4

Any person who knowingly transmits a false report to the department commits the offense of disorderly conduct under Ch. 720, § 5/26.1(a)(7). A violation of this provision is a Class 4 felony.

Massachusetts

Failure to Report
Gen. Laws Ch. 119, § 51A

Any mandatory reporter who fails to report shall be punished by a fine of no more than $1,000.

Any mandated reporter who has knowledge of child abuse or neglect that resulted in serious bodily injury to or death of a child and willfully fails to report the abuse or neglect shall be punished by a fine of up to $5,000 or imprisonment for no more than 2 1/2 years, or by both, and, upon a guilty finding or a continuance without a finding, the court shall notify any appropriate professional licensing authority of the mandated reporter's violation of this paragraph.

False Reporting
Gen. Laws Ch. 119, § 51A

Whoever knowingly and willfully files a frivolous report of child abuse or neglect under this section shall be punished by:

- A fine of no more than $2,000 for the first offense
- Imprisonment for no more than 6 months and a fine of no more than $2,000 for the second offense
- Imprisonment for no more than 2 1/2 years and a fine of no more than $2,000 for the third and subsequent offenses

New York

Failure to Report
Soc. Serv. Law § 420

Any mandatory reporter who willfully fails to report as required shall be guilty of a Class A misdemeanor.

Any mandatory reporter who knowingly and willfully fails to report as required shall be civilly liable for the damages proximately caused by such failure.

False Reporting
Penal Law § 240.50(4)

A person is guilty of falsely reporting an incident in the third degree when, knowing the information reported, conveyed, or circulated to be false or baseless, he or she reports, by word or action, an alleged occurrence or condition of child abuse or maltreatment that did not in fact occur or exist to:

- The statewide central register of child abuse and maltreatment
- Any person required to report cases of suspected child abuse or maltreatment, knowing that the person is required to report such cases, and with the intent that such an alleged occurrence be reported to the statewide central register

Falsely reporting an incident in the third degree is a Class A misdemeanor.

Texas

Failure to Report
Fam. Code § 261.109

A person commits an offense if the person has cause to believe that a child's physical or mental health or welfare has been or may be adversely affected by abuse or neglect and knowingly fails to report in accordance with the reporting laws.

An offense under this section is a Class A misdemeanor, except that the offense is a State jail felony if it is shown on the trial of the offense that the child was a person with mental retardation who resided in a State-supported living center, the medical assistance program for persons with mental retardation component of the Rio Grande State Center, or a facility licensed under Chapter 252, Health and Safety Code, and the actor knew that the child had suffered serious bodily injury as a result of the abuse or neglect.

False Reporting
Fam. Code § 261.107

A person commits an offense if, with the intent to deceive, he or she knowingly makes a report of child abuse or neglect that is false. An offense under this subsection is:

- A State jail felony
- A felony of the third degree if the person has previously been convicted under this section

A person who is convicted of an offense under this section shall:

- Pay any reasonable attorney's fees incurred by the person who was falsely accused of abuse or neglect
- Be liable to the State for a civil penalty of $1,000

References

Bolen, R. (2011). Incidence and prevalence of child sexual abuse. *Child sexual abuse: Its scope and our failure* (pp. 65-90). Boston: Kluwer Academic Publishers.

Boy Scouts of America. (2005). *How to protect your children from child abuse: A parent's guide*. Retrieved from www.scouting.org/filestore/pdf/46-014.pdf.

Boys & Girls Clubs of The Peninsula. (2013). *Crisis management plan*. Retrieved from http://www.bgcp.org/WP/Linked_Documents/forms/BGCP%20CRISIS%20MANAGEMENT%20PLAN.pdf.

Broman-Fulks, J.J., Ruggiero, K.J., Hanson, R.F., Smith, D.W., Resnick, H.S., Kilpatrick, D.G., & Saunders, B.E. (2007). Sexual assault disclosure in relation to adolescent mental health: Results from the National Survey of Adolescents. *Journal of Clinical Child and Adolescent Psychology, 36(2)I,* 260-266.

Child Welfare Information Gateway (1999). *Prior abuse reported by inmates and probationers.* Washington, DC: U.S. Department of Health and Human Services, Children's Bureau.

Child Welfare Information Gateway (2008). *Long-term consequences of child abuse and neglect.* Washington, DC: U.S. Department of Health and Human Services, Children's Bureau.

Child Welfare Information Gateway. (2012). *Mandatory reporters of child abuse and neglect: Summary of state laws.* Washington, DC: U.S. Department of Health and Human Services, Children's Bureau.

Elliott, M. (1995) Child sexual abuse prevention: What offenders tell us. *Child Abuse & Neglect, Vol. 19(5)*, 579-594.

Finkelhor, D., & Jones, L. (2004). Explanations for the decline in child sexual abuse cases. *Juvenile Justice Bulletin.* Retrieved from Office of Juvenile Justice and Delinquency Prevention. Retrieved from http://www.ojp.usdoj.gov/ojjdp.

Finkelhor, D., & Ormrod, R. (2001). Factors in the underreporting of crimes against juveniles. *Child Maltreatment, 6(3)*, 219-229.

Finkelhor, D. Ormrod, R., & Turner, H. (2007). Poly-victimization: A neglected component in child victimization. *Child Abuse & Neglect,* 31:7-26.

Finkelhor, D., Turner, H., Ormrod, R., Hamby, S., & Kracke, K. (2009). Children's exposure to violence: A comprehensive national survey. *Juvenile Justice Bulletin.* Retrieved from Office of Juvenile Justice and Delinquency Prevention. Retrieved from http://www.ojp.usdoj.gov/ojjdp.

Freeh Sporkin & Sullivan, LLP. (2012). *Report of the special investigative counsel regarding the actions of the Pennsylvania State University related to the child sexual abuse committed by Gerald A. Sandusky.* Special Investigations Task Force, The Pennsylvania State University's Board of Trustees, Pennsylvania State University.

Havig, K. (2008). The health care experiences of adult survivors of child sexual abuse: A systematic review of evidence on sensitive practice. *Trauma, Violence, & Abuse, 9(1)*, 19-33.

Johnson, R. (2008). Advances in understanding and treating child sexual abuse: Implications for research and policy. *Family & Community Health, 31(1S)*, S24-S31.

Lanning, K. (2010). *Child molesters: A behavioral analysis for professionals investigating the sexual exploitation of children.* Fifth ed. National Center for Missing and Exploited Children. Office of Juvenile Justice and Delinquincy Prevention. Office of Justice Programs, US Department of Justice. Federal Bureau of Investigation.

National Association of Adult Survivors of Child Abuse. (2009). *Child sexual abuse accommodation syndrome.* Retrieved April 3, 2013, from http://www.naasca.org/2011-Articles/060111-ChildSexAbuseAccommodation-Syndrome.htm.

Newlin, C., Book, L., Book, R., Moore, T., & Sewell, J. (2012). *Recommendations to the Amateur Athletic Union from the youth protection and adult/volunteer screening task forces.* Retrieved from http://image.aausports.org/dnn/pdf/TFreportfinal.pdf.

Office of the Attorney General. (2006). *The Attorney General's report on criminal history background checks.* Washington, DC: U.S. Government Printing Office. Retrieved from http://www.justice.gov/olp/ag_bgchecks_report.pdf.

Parent, S. (2011). Disclosure of sexual abuse in sport organizations: A case study. *Journal of Child Sexual Abuse, 20(3)*, 322-337.

Saul, J. & Audage, N.C. (2007). *Preventing child sexual abuse within youth-serving organizations: Getting started on policies and procedures.* Atlanta, GA: Centers for Disease Control and Prevention, National Center for Injury Prevention and Control.

Security Designed into New and Remodeled Facilities in Security Magazine, August 7, 2008.

Smith, D.W., Letourneay, E.J., Saunders, B.E., Kilpatrick, D.G., Resnick, H.S., & Best, C.L. (2000). Delay in disclosure of childhood rape: Results from a national survey. *Child Abuse & Neglect, 24(2)*, 273-287.

Sullivan, J., & Beech, A. (2002). Professional perpetrators: Sex offenders who use their employment to target and sexually abuse the children with whom they work. *Child Abuse Review, 11*, 153-167.

Sullivan, J., & Beech, A. (2004). A comparative study of demographic data relating to intra-and extra-familial child sexual abusers and professional perpetrators. *Journal of Sexual Aggression, 10(1)*, 39-50.

Additional Sources

Helpful Websites:

Stop It Now – www.stopitnow.org

Darkness to Light – www.darkness2light.org

Child Welfare Information Gateway – www.childwelfare.gov

Department of Health and Human Services – www.hhs.gov

Children's Bureau – www.acf.hhs.gov/programs/cb

Crimes Against Children Research Center (UNH) – www.unh.edu/ccrc

Staff Screening Tool Kit – www.nationalserviceresources.org/files/r3300-staff-screening-tool-kit.pdf

Safe 4 Athletes – www.safe4athletes.org

The National Center for Victims of Crime – www.victimsofcrime.org

The National Crime Prevention Council – www.ncpc.org

Training for Children – www.srtell.org

Related Scholarly Sources:

The Scope of the Problem

1. Myers, J. (2011). The APSAC Handbook on Child Maltreatment. 3rd edition

2. Finkelhor, D. & Jones, L. (2004). Explanations for the decline in child sexual abuse cases. US Department of Justice. Office of Justice Programs. Office of Juvenile Justice and Delinquency Programs.

3. Ullman, S. (2007). Relationship to perpetrator, disclosure, social reactions, and PTSD symptoms in child sexual abuse survivors. Journal of Child Sexual Abuse, Vol. 16(1), 19-36.

4. Pereda, N., Guilera, G., Forns, M., Gomez-Benito, J. (2009). The international epidemiology of child sexual abuse: A continuation of Finkelhor. Child Abuse & Neglect, Vol. 33, 331-342.

Perpetrators

5. Elliott, M. (1995). Child sexual abuse prevention: What offenders tell us. Child Abuse & Neglect, Vol. 19(5), 579-594.

6. Bagley, C. & Pritchard, C. (2000). Criminality and violence in intra-and extra-familial child sex abusers in a 2 year cohort of convicted perpetrators. Child Abuse Review, Vol. 9, 264-274.

7. Abel, G., Wiegel, M., Jordan, A., Harlow, N., Hsu, Y., Martinez, M. (2012). Development and validation of classification models to

identify hidden child molesters applying for child service organizations. Children & Youth Services Review, Vol. 34(7), 1378-1389.

Victim Impact

8. Dube, S., Anda, R., Whitfield, C., Brown, D., Felitti, V., Dong, M., Giles, W. (2005). Long-term consequences of childhood sexual abuse by gender of victim. American Journal of Preventative Medicine, Vol. 28(5), 430-480.

Reporting/Disclosure

9. Alaggia, R. (2004). Many ways of telling: expanding conceptualizations of child sexual abuse disclosure. Child Abuse & Neglect, Vol. 28, 1213-1227.

10. Webster, S., O'Toole, A., O'Toole, R., Lucal, B. (2005). Over-reporting and underreporting of child abuse: Teacher's use of professional discretion. Child Abuse & Neglect, Vol. 29, 1281-1296.

11. Parent, S. (2011). Case studies: Disclosure of sexual abuse in sport organizations: A case study. Journal of Child Sexual Abuse, Vol. 20, 322-337.

General Prevention

12. Wurtele, S. (2009). Child sexual abuse prevention: Preventing sexual abuse of children in the twenty-first century: Preparing for challenges and opportunities. Journal of Child Sexual Abuse, Vol. 18, 1-18.

Poly-Victimization

13. Finkelhor, D., Ormrod, R. & Turner, H. (2007) Poly-Victimization: A Neglected Component in Child Victimization. Child Abuse & Neglect, 31:7-26